Health Care Finance, Economics, and Policy for Nurses

Betty Rambur, PhD, RN, is a professor of nursing and health policy at the University of Vermont (UVM). From 2000 to 2009, she served as an academic dean at UVM, where she led the merger of the School of Nursing and the School of Health Sciences to establish the College of Nursing and Health Sciences. These experiences have built on Dr. Rambur's substantive leadership history in health policy and finance. From 1991 to 1995, she led the statewide health financing reform effort in North Dakota. An RN, Dr. Rambur received her PhD in nursing from Rush University in Chicago, Illinois. She maintains an active research program focused on health services, quality, workforce, and ethics. She has led or participated in research, education, and public service grants exceeding $2 million, is the author of about 40 published articles, and has made numerous invited presentations on her research, health care economics and policy, and leadership development. In 2007, her research was honored by Sigma Theta Tau International. Dr. Rambur is also an accomplished teacher in both classroom and online venues. In May 2013, she received the UVM Graduate Student Senate Excellence in Teaching Award, and in November 2013, she received the prestigious Sloan Consortium Excellence in Online Teaching and Learning Award. Her teaching expertise includes the organization, finance, and policy of health care, payment reform, and evidence-based practice. Dr. Rambur was appointed to Vermont's Green Mountain Care Board by Vermont's Governor Peter Shumlin in August 2013. The five-member Green Mountain Care Board is a quasi-judicial body. It oversees Vermont's financing, payment, and delivery reform and holds board regulatory, innovation, and evaluation authority.

Health Care Finance, Economics, and Policy for Nurses

A Foundational Guide

Betty Rambur, PhD, RN

SPRINGER PUBLISHING COMPANY
NEW YORK

Springer Publishing Company, LLC
11 West 42nd Street
New York, NY 10036
www.springerpub.com

Acquisitions Editor: Elizabeth Nieginski
Production Editor: Kris Parrish
Composition: Exeter Premedia Services Private Ltd.

ISBN: 978-0-8261-2322-0
e-book ISBN: 978-0-8261-2323-7
Instructor's Manual: 978-0-8261-6925-9
Instructor's PowerPoints: 978-0-8261-6927-3
Student Study Guide: 978-0-8261-6926-6
Instructor's Test Bank: 978-0-8261-6928-0

Instructor's materials are available to qualified adopters by contacting textbook@springerpub.com.

15 16 17 18 / 5 4 3 2 1

The author and the publisher of this Work have made every effort to use sources believed to be reliable to provide information that is accurate and compatible with the standards generally accepted at the time of publication. Because medical science is continually advancing, our knowledge base continues to expand. Therefore, as new information becomes available, changes in procedures become necessary. We recommend that the reader always consult current research and specific institutional policies before performing any clinical procedure. The author and publisher shall not be liable for any special, consequential, or exemplary damages resulting, in whole or in part, from the readers' use of, or reliance on, the information contained in this book. The publisher has no responsibility for the persistence or accuracy of URLs for external or third-party Internet websites referred to in this publication and does not guarantee that any content on such websites is, or will remain, accurate or appropriate.

Library of Congress Cataloging-in-Publication Data

Rambur, Betty, author.
Health care finance, economics, and policy for nurses : a foundational guide / Betty Rambur.
    p. ; cm.
  Includes bibliographical references and index.
  ISBN 978-0-8261-2322-0—ISBN 978-0-8261-2323-7 (e-book)
  I. Title.
  [DNLM: 1. Healthcare Financing—Nurses' Instruction.   2. Healthcare Financing—Problems and Exercises.   3. Decision Making—Nurses' Instruction.   4. Decision Making—Problems and Exercises.   5. Health Care Costs—Nurses' Instruction.   6. Health Care Costs—Problems and Exercises.   7. Health Policy—Nurses' Instruction.   8. Health Policy—Problems and Exercises. W 74.1]
  RT86.7
  362.17'30681—dc23
                                                                          2014049307

Printed in the United States of America by Bang Printing.

To my students, whose questions encourage me to try ever harder to make finance, economics, and policy understandable and useful.

CONTENTS

FOREWORD

As we travel around the country to promote nursing leadership, we hear a familiar refrain from health care leaders: Nurses bring strategic planning skills, sound clinical knowledge, and an ability to respond to crisis to boards and policy-making tables, but nurses must also possess business acumen to be considered for top leadership positions. They must understand policy making, negotiation and influence, and health finance, including the ability to read a financial statement.

That's why *Health Care Finance, Economics, and Policy for Nurses: A Foundational Guide* offers crucial knowledge to prepare nurses in RN-to-BSN and second degree programs to serve in leadership positions. As Betty Rambur eloquently explains, health care financing, economics, and policy making are foundational nursing knowledge in the 21st century, a sentiment clearly stated in the landmark Institute of Medicine (IOM) report, *The Future of Nursing: Leading Change, Advancing Health* (Institute of Medicine, 2011). Being exposed to Rambur's book in nursing school will help to ensure that nurses are knowledgeable in business and finance skills and understand the importance of pursuing leadership positions to better serve patients, families, and communities.

Our organizations, the Robert Wood Johnson Foundation and AARP, are spearheading The Future of Nursing: Campaign for Action, a national initiative to improve health through nursing by advancing the recommendations in the IOM report. We are delighted that 19 national nursing organizations have joined us in forming the Nurses on Boards Coalition to place 10,000 nurses on boards by 2020. Nurses bring unique competencies to boards and policy-making tables, including community orientation, collaboration, organizational awareness, accountability, team leadership, relationship building, negotiation skills, and professionalism. They also have knowledge and skills to track measures of quality, safety, and customer satisfaction in health care delivery and performance. Equally important, nurses bring the consumer's voice to the fore and are driven by a lifelong commitment to human caring—and that should be the cornerstone of all efforts to improve health and health care. Nurses are the reality check in any decisions being made that affect the delivery of care and the promotion of health.

However, few nurses serve on boards: The American Hospital Association estimates that nurses fill 6% of board seats, compared with 20% for physicians (AHA, 2010). *Health Care Finance, Economics, and Policy for Nurses: A Foundational Guide* will help to change that by teaching nursing students early on that business and finance skills are a requisite for their careers. It should be required reading in every school of nursing in the United States. We hope that faculty members will embrace this book, and that nursing students who read the book will be inspired to pursue leadership roles and make it their goal to sit at tables where they can truly effect change and advance health.

Susan B. Hassmiller, PhD, RN, FAAN
Senior Adviser for Nursing, Robert Wood Johnson Foundation
Director, Campaign for Action

Susan Reinhard, PhD, RN, FAAN
Senior Vice President and Director, AARP Public Policy Institute
Chief Strategist, Center to Champion Nursing in America

REFERENCES

American Hospital Association (AHA). (2011). *AHA hospital statistics, 2011 edition.* Chicago, IL: Author.

Institute of Medicine (IOM). (2011). *The future of nursing: Leading change, advancing health.* Washington, DC: National Academies Press.

PREFACE

Health care financing, economics, and policy are foundational to nursing knowledge in the 21st century. *The Essentials of Baccalaureate Education for Professional Nursing Practice* by the American Association of Colleges of Nursing (AACN, 2008) states, "Baccalaureate generalist nurses are designers, coordinators, and managers of care" (p. 9). These skills, in turn, depend on sound understanding of health financing, economics, politics, and policies, as well as new systems of care fueled by emerging payment models. To design, coordinate, and manage care as the *Essentials* require, nurses must understand the Affordable Care Act of 2010 and its implications for patients, nursing practice, and health care. We must be agile enough to work with a range of payment and delivery reform models—from fee-for-service–based, patient-centered medical homes; accountable care organizations with or without shared saving programs; and pay for performance to post–fee-for-service models, such as like bundled payments and global budgets. We must understand why hospitals are merging, and what this means to cost, outcomes, and nursing practice. This text provides you, the reader, with the knowledge to artfully navigate this terrain through foundational understanding of the finance, economics, and policies that shape health reform, as well as our daily lives as nurses and citizens.

This knowledge is so important that one entire "Essential" in *The Essentials of Baccalaureate Education* is devoted to it: "Healthcare Policy, Finance and Regulatory Environments" (Essential V). This "Essential" notes, "Healthcare policies including financial and regulatory policies, directly and indirectly influence nursing practice as well as the nature and functioning of the health care system....The baccalaureate-educated graduate will have a solid understanding of the broader context of health care, including how patient care services are organized and financed, and how reimbursement is structured" (AACN, 2008, p. 20).

Yet many nursing programs struggle to incorporate this content in meaningful, tangible ways—a gap that *Health Care Finance, Economics, and Policy for Nurses: A Foundational Guide* is designed to address. Previous generations of nurses were not fully schooled in the issues of finance and, instead, were socialized to believe that nurses should not think about resources when considering patient care. Nor has the public fully expected nurses to think about finances and economics. Perhaps, we—as nurses—often do not even desire economic acumen, having from the beginning chosen a profession in which we perceive people, not money, to be at the center. Paradoxically, this creates tensions because financial incentives and disincentives shape individual and organizational behavior. Economics fuels the health care system, and finances etch every element of the health care workplace. Economics and patient care are inexorably linked.

So, leaving the finances and politics for someone else to worry about is no longer a viable or even ethical approach, catalyzing great urgency for this foundational nursing knowledge in the era of reform. Readers of this text will be well prepared to navigate the contemporary care landscape, armed with an understanding of ethical, patient-centered care within a resource- constrained environment. Readers will also be prepared to use the language and actions of influence—that is, the language of finance, economics, and policy.

The language and actions of influence are also necessary to redesign the health care system toward the 2001 goals of the Institute of Medicine (IOM) detailed in *Crossing the Quality Chasm: A New Health System for the 21st Century*: safe, effective, patient-centered, timely, efficient, and equitable patient care. Such redesign cannot happen with knowledge and skills developed in an episodic, fee-for-service, acute care–oriented world. As Einstein sagely notes, "We cannot solve our problems with the same thinking we used when we created them." Fortunately, finance and economics are new thinking for many nurses. Thus, knowledge of economics, finance, and policy, joined with more traditional nursing knowledge, provides nurses with binocular vision; nurses are uniquely positioned to hold a view of the individual patient and family simultaneously with consideration of overarching population health goals and financial impacts on society at large. This is an enormously complex skill set, yet nurses—with knowledge of patients and systems—are ideally suited for the important social responsibility of knitting together the needs of the individual and society at large within a landscape that considers health, health care, cost, and quality. The central role of each and every nurse—yes, you—cannot be overstated. Fraher, Ricketts, Lefebvre, and Newton (2013) note that "because of sheer numbers—the U.S. health care system employs 2.7 million registered nurses—it is nurses who are arguably in the most pivotal position to drive systems change" (p. 1812). Society needs your clear-sighted nursing vision in this time of rapid change.

In addition to Essential V, there are other Essentials directly supported by material in this text. For example, Essentials II.3—"Demonstrate an awareness of complex organizational systems"—and II.4—"Demonstrate a basic understanding of organizational structure, mission, vision, philosophy, and values" (AACN, 2008, p. 14)—are addressed in Chapters 9 and 10 of this text. Other elements of this text provide important background material that can help you make connections among different domains of study and practice. Chapter 5, for example, details the role of information through the lens of economic, policy, and patient perspectives. In so doing, it provides supportive material for Essential IV, "Information Management and Application of Patient Care Technology: #12: Participate in evaluation of information systems in practice settings through policy and procedure development" (AACN, 2008, p. 19). Additional examples of links among text content and *Essentials of Baccalaureate Education* may be found in Table P.1.

Table P.1
Relationship Among *Essentials of Baccalaureate Education for Professional Nursing Practice* and Text Content

The Essentials of Baccalaureate Education for Professional Nursing Practice	Text Support, by Criterion
Essential I.5: Apply knowledge of social and cultural factors to the care of diverse populations.	Indirect
Essential I.6: Engage in ethical reasoning and actions to provide leadership in promoting advocacy, collaboration, and social justice as a socially responsible citizen.	Direct
Essential I.7: Integrate the knowledge and methods of a variety of disciplines to inform decision making.	Direct
Essential I.8: Demonstrate tolerance for the ambiguity and unpredictability of the world and its effect on the health care system.	Indirect
Essential II.1: Apply leadership concepts, skills, and decision making in the provision of high quality nursing care, health care team coordination, and the oversight and accountability for care delivery in a variety of settings.	Direct
Essential II.3: Demonstrate an awareness of complex organizational systems.	Direct

(continued)

Table P-1 (*continued*)

Relationship Among *Essentials of Baccalaureate Education for Professional Nursing Practice* and Text Content

The Essentials of Baccalaureate Education for Professional Nursing Practice	Text Support, by Criterion
Essential II.4: Demonstrate a basic understanding of organizational structure, mission, vision, philosophy, and values.	Direct
Essential II.5: Participate in quality and patient safety initiatives, recognizing that these are complex system issues, which involve individuals, families, groups, communities, populations, and other members of the health care team.	Indirect
Essential II.11: Employ principles of quality improvement, health care policy, and cost-effectiveness to assist in the development and initiation of effective plans for the microsystem and/ or system-wide practice improvements that will improve the quality of health care delivery.	Direct
Essential II.12: Participate in the development and implementation of imaginative and creative strategies to enable systems of change.	Direct
Essential III.8: Acquire an understanding of the process for how nursing and related health care quality and safety measures are developed, validated, and endorsed.	Indirect
Essential IV.7: Recognize the role of information technology in improving patient care outcomes and creating a safe care environment.	Direct
Essential IV.11: Recognize that redesign of workflow and care processes should precede implementation of care technology to facilitate nursing practice.	Indirect
Essential IV:12: Participate in evaluation of information systems in practice settings through policy and procedure development.	Indirect
Essential V.1: Demonstrate basic knowledge of health care policy, finance, and regulatory environments, including local, state, national, and global health care trends.	Direct
Essential V.2: Describe how health care is organized and financed, including the implications of business principals, such as patient and system cost factors.	Direct
Essential V.3: Compare the benefits and limitations of the major forms of reimbursement on the delivery of health care services.	Direct

(*continued*)

Table P-1 (*continued*)

Relationship Among *Essentials of Baccalaureate Education for Professional Nursing Practice* and Text Content

The Essentials of Baccalaureate Education for Professional Nursing Practice	Text Support, by Criterion
Essential V.4: Examine legislative and regulatory processes relevant to the provision of health care.	Direct
Essential V.5: Describe state and national statutes, rules, and regulations that authorize and define professional nursing practice.	Indirect
Essential V.6: Explore the impact of sociocultural, economic, legal, and political factors influencing health care delivery and practice.	Direct
Essential V.7: Examine the roles and responsibilities of the regulatory agencies and their effort on patient care quality, workplace safety, and the scope of nursing and other health professionals' practice.	Direct
Essential V.8: Discuss the implications of health care policy on issues of access, equity, affordability, and social justice in health care delivery.	Direct
Essential V.9: Use an ethical framework to evaluate the impact of social policies on health care, especially for vulnerable populations.	Direct
Essential V.10: Articulate, through a nursing perspective, issues concerning health care delivery on decision makers within health care organizations and other policy arenas.	Direct
Essential V.11: Participate as a nursing professional in political processes and grassroots legislative efforts to influence health care policy.	Direct
Essential VI.4: Contribute the unique nursing perspective to interprofessional teams to optimize patient outcomes.	Indirect
Essential VI.5: Demonstrate appropriate teambuilding and collaborative strategies when working with interprofessional teams.	Indirect
Essential VII.10: Collaborate with others to develop an intervention plan that takes into account determinates of health, available resources, and the range of activities that contribute to health and the prevention of illness, injury, disability, and premature death.	Indirect

(*continued*)

Table P-1 (*continued*)

Relationship Among *Essentials of Baccalaureate Education for
Professional Nursing Practice* and Text Content

The Essentials of Baccalaureate Education for Professional Nursing Practice	Text Support, by Criterion
Essential VII.11: Participate in clinical prevention and population-focused interventions with attention to effectiveness, efficiency, cost-effectiveness, and equity.	Indirect
Essential VII.12: Advocate for social justice, including a commitment to the health of vulnerable populations and the elimination of health disparities.	Direct
Essential VII.13: Use evaluation results to influence the delivery of care, deployment, and resources, and to provide input into the development of policies to promote health and prevent disease.	Direct
Essential VIII.1: Demonstrate the professional standards of moral, ethical, and legal conduct.	Direct
Essential VIII.2: Assume accountability for personal and professional behaviors.	Direct
Essential VIII.3: Promote the image of nursing by modeling the values and articulating the knowledge, skills, and attitudes of the nursing profession.	Direct
Essential VIII.5: Demonstrate an appreciation of the history of and contemporary issues in nursing and their impact on current nursing practice.	Direct
Essential VIII.11: Access interprofessional and intraprofessional resources to resolve ethical and other practice dilemmas.	Indirect
Essential IX.3: Implement holistic, patient-centered care that reflects an understanding of human growth and development, pathophysiology, pharmacology, medical management, and nursing management across the health-illness continuum, across the lifespan, and in all health care settings.	Indirect
Essential IX.4: Communicate effectively with all members of the health care team, including the patient and the patient's support network.	Indirect
Essential IX.5: Deliver compassionate, patient-centered, evidence-based care that respects patient and family preferences.	Indirect

(*continued*)

Table P-1 (*continued*)

Relationship Among *Essentials of Baccalaureate Education for Professional Nursing Practice* and Text Content

The Essentials of Baccalaureate Education for Professional Nursing Practice	Text Support, by Criterion
Essential IX.8: Implement evidence-based nursing interventions as appropriate for managing the acute and chronic care of patients, and promoting health across the lifespan.	Indirect
Essential IX.11: Provide nursing care based on evidence that contributes to safe and high quality patient outcomes within health care microsystems.	Indirect
Essential IX.12: Create a safe care environment that results in high-quality patient outcomes.	Indirect
Essential IX.14: Demonstrate clinical judgment and accountability for patient outcomes when delegating to and supervising other members of the health care team.	Indirect
Essential IX.22: Demonstrate tolerance for the ambiguity and unpredictability of the world and its effect on the health care system relating to nursing practice.	Direct

In 2010, IOM promulgated another set of important recommendations in *The Future of Nursing: Leading Change, Advancing Health. Health Care Financing, Economics, and Policy for Nurses: A Fundamental Guide* directly supports its key recommendations, for example, the call for the health care system to serve society better through opportunities for "nurses to assume leadership positions and to serve as full partners in health care redesign and improvement efforts" (p. 1). To be a full partner requires solid grounding in "how the money works"—a core focus of this text—given that finances are a sort of oxygen feeding elements of the health care system. Notably, what is fed will grow; what is not financially fed will wither.

The 2010 IOM recommendations assume substantial payment and delivery literacy, for example, the recommendation that "The Centers for Medicare and Medicaid Innovation should support the development and evaluation of models of payment and care delivery that use nurses in an expanded and leadership capacity to improve health outcomes and reduce costs" (p. 11). To attain this outcome, nurses must be conversant with the payment models defined in this text and recognize meaningful potential adoptions in their own practice or leadership role.

Nurses have filled many bedside and managerial roles for decades. Yet another key IOM 2010 recommendation envisions more comprehensive leadership roles for nurses: "Public, private, and governmental health care decision makers at every level should include representation from nurses on boards" (p. 14). Nonetheless, many nurses are unfamiliar with how to access board roles, are unaware that they exist, or do not have governance or regulatory aspirations. To fill this gap, this text—unique among contemporary materials—offers two chapters devoted to developing nurse awareness of the structures, processes, and appointment avenues for governance, advisory, and regulatory boards. In accessing board membership, one may consider Florence Nightingale's apt dictum on what a nurse must keep in mind: "...not, how can I always do this right thing myself, but...how can I provide for this right thing to always be done?" (cited in Ulrich, 1992, p. 38).

Finally, although clinical ethics is a domain most nurses and nursing programs are prepared to consider, the interplay among ethics, economics, and health reform is not. Indeed, the area of ethinomics, the intersection of ethics and economics, is uncharted territory for many nurses. This text is designed to provide nurses with the ethical tools to consider the intersection of the individual and population care, overtreatment and undertreatment, metric-driven harm, and the economic impact of clinical decision making on equality of opportunity in other domains of individual and population life. Although there are no easy answers, the hope guiding this text development is that the nurse will have better questions and heightened awareness, perhaps even seeing ethical dilemmas in what once seemed commonplace practice. Such discernment builds moral muscle and is the first step toward heightened ethical efficacy and moral health. Taken as a whole, health economics, finance, and politics, applied from bedside to boardroom, locally to internationally, enables nurses to assure that the right thing is always done, just as Florence Nightingale advised.

How This Book Is Organized

Chapters 1 and 2 provide an introduction to health economics and develop foundational terms and concepts, such as financing, reimbursement, and payment. The reader is asked to be patient with these materials, as they form a sort of foundation to the broader health care story and nursing practice. Understanding the evolution of financing, reimbursement, and payment within the U.S. health care system, including a pattern of potential solutions leading to unintended consequences, helps the reader place the contemporary health system within a broader historic milieu. This historic understanding is important, as many valued as well as problematic aspects of health care are rooted in the past; such understanding enables you to better navigate change as well as lead it.

Chapter 3 provides an overview of payment reform models, which are then explicated in Chapters 4 through 6 by contrasting the more familiar classic free markets and health care markets. This knowledge thereby provides a context for understanding aspects of the Affordable Care Act and state reform efforts, both now and in the future. Chapters 7 and 8 interlace these issues with ethical perspectives and models for ethical decision making.

You are now prepared to apply what you have learned to leadership positions on boards and to the policy process. Thus, Chapters 9 through 11 offer practical, tangible advice on how this more profound sense of self can be used by the nurse in governance and policy settings. Chapter 12 offers closing thoughts on how to embrace continuous learning in these areas to ensure that you bring your knowledge into the world in vital, immediate, impactful ways throughout your entire professional career.

Each chapter includes vignettes that illustrate complex economic and financial concepts in scenarios that are familiar to everyday life. These vignettes offer a bridge between your existing common knowledge and financial and economic material that may otherwise seem like a foreign language in a foreign land. The approach is designed to help the reader successfully translate known concepts and processes to new financial, economic, policy, and regulatory terrain. Each chapter closes with thought questions to ponder and explore with classmates, peers, and faculty. Again, the intention is to ensure that you are conversant—and, over time, fluent—in the language and tools of finance, economics, and politics. Chapters are augmented with quiz reviews that serve as checkpoints to help you assess your acquisition of this new knowledge. **Qualified instructors may obtain access to ancillary materials, such as a sample syllabus, test bank, student supplements, and PowerPoints, by contacting** *textbook@springerpub.com.*

Summary and Conclusion

The goal of *Health Care Financing, Economics, and Policy for Nurses: A Foundational Guide* is to help you understand health finance and economics, and powerfully incorporate this knowledge across a span that ranges from direct patient care to positions with national or even international impact. Without this understanding, nurses cannot find solid ground for leadership, and much of what is happening in the practice setting simply will not make sense. With it, nurses can change the world. Enjoy!

REFERENCES

American Association of Colleges of Nursing. (2008). *The essentials of baccalaureate education for professional nursing practice*. Washington, DC: Author.

Fraher, E., Ricketts, T., Lefebvre, A., & Newton, W. (2013). The role of academic health centers and their partners in retooling the existing workforce to practice in a transformed setting. *Academic Medicine, 88*, 1812–1816. doi:10.1097/ACM.0000000000000024

Institute of Medicine. (2001). *Crossing the quality chasm: A new health system for the 21st century*. Washington, DC: National Academy of Sciences.

Institute of Medicine. (2010). *The future of nursing: Leading change, advancing health*. Washington, DC: National Academy of Sciences.

Ulrich, B. (1992). *Leadership and management according to Florence Nightingale*. Norwalk, CT: Appleton and Lange.

ACKNOWLEDGMENTS

This book would not have been possible without a great deal of help and encouragement from others. Elizabeth Nieginski and Springer Publishing Company's initial interest in the idea for this text, and their encouragement along the way, have been invaluable. William Patrick Rambur's technical support and assistance in the development of ancillary materials was a saving grace. Thanks, son! Jill Mattuck Tarule's conceptually elegant insights have created a more readable text, and her time and thoughtful edits are deeply appreciated. Two states, North Dakota and Vermont, have given me the opportunity to lead health reform within and beyond their borders. I am very grateful to the citizens of these states and my colleagues in these reform endeavors. You have taught me so much! And finally, special thanks to my friend with a cottage by the sea, whose love and support offered welcome refuge for a writer.

ACKNOWLEDGMENTS

THE CONTEXT OF HEALTH CARE AND HEALTH CARE REFORM

Section I, comprising Chapters 1, 2, and 3, provides foundational background that is essential for you to be able to successfully navigate contemporary health care. Chapter 1 describes basics of health finance and economics, rather like an alphabet that is necessary for reading and writing in the health care landscape. Perhaps similar to first learning a new alphabet, it can be a bit tedious. Be patient. These terms and ideas are a language of power and influence that you will need to maximize your career opportunities.

Chapter 2 details the evolution of the U.S. health care system. Knowledge of this history is essential to understanding many contemporary issues, including health reform. This is because many reform elements are strategies to address unintended consequences of previous health care policies and accidents of history.

Chapter 3 pulls this information together to illustrate the ways payment reform—the way physicians, hospitals, home health care agencies, and other organizations are paid—shapes your daily work life and how you can use this knowledge to influence positive change. So, let us begin with Chapter 1 and sort out foundational concepts like financing, economics, and reimbursement, as well as become familiar with insurance-related aspects of the Affordable Care Act of 2010.

1

WHAT IS HEALTH ECONOMICS AND WHY IS IT IMPORTANT TO NURSES?

CHAPTER 1 PROVIDES an introduction to health economics and its influence on contemporary nursing and health care. Following completion of this chapter, you will be able to

- Define health economics and differentiate it from related concepts such as health financing and reimbursement
- Describe how health care is paid for in the United States
- Illustrate elements related to payment of health care services, such as third-party payers and commercial insurance
- Identify insurance-related elements of the Affordable Care Act (ACA)

1964: Mary Jane is excited to be in sixth grade. Her first day of school was magnificent! As her mother putters in the kitchen to make Mary Jane's after-school snack, she settles in to read her history text. "America is the land of endless opportunity and unlimited natural resources," announces the text's opening statement. Reading these lines, Mary Jane smiles, thinking, "How wonderful it is to live in a world in which there are no limits!"

2014: Will is excited to be in sixth grade. Knowing that his mother will not be home from work for several hours, he grabs a snack as he opens his integrated humanities text. Glancing through the headings, he sees that many issues of the day are woven into the chapters: global climate change, the economy, and unsustainable industries that range from U.S. business practices to health care. The book suggests that new ways of thinking are needed to solve these problems, many of which are rooted in issues of scarce resources. Pondering, Will hopes he is up to this challenge.

Nurses care about their patients. Some nurses, who like Mary Jane were imprinted with the myth of endless abundance, believe that there should be no limits on what is done for patients. Indeed, earlier generations of nurses, physicians, and other providers were socialized to believe that it is unethical to even consider the cost of care when making treatment decisions.

Contemporary nurses know better. They know that resources both within and beyond heath care are not unlimited. They know that choices among alternatives will be, and need to be, made. What nurses often lack is the tools to help them think about ethical and practical ways in which scarce resources are managed, allocated, and used to maximize value and outcomes. This competency is an essential element of contemporary nursing practice, because the societal transition from a world of certainty and perceived abundance to one of multiplicity and perceived scarcity illustrated in the opening scenarios characterizes today's health care delivery. Health care is too expensive, fragmented, and characterized by irregular quality. Unfortunately, many health professionals have been educated as if the world they will be working in is Mary Jane's world of 1964.

Luckily, there is a whole discipline—complete with theories, research, and practical applications—that provides foundational nursing knowledge in the contemporary era of health reform. This discipline is economics. The overarching field of economics is concerned with the question of how goods and services are produced, organized, and delivered to maximize efficiency and value. The emphasis on value is important: Economics is not necessarily concerned with *more*, but *better*, a concern that nurses share as a fundamental value.

THEORETICAL ECONOMIC APPROACHES

There are different theoretical approaches to economics. One approach most nurses have been exposed to since elementary school is *classic free market* or *laissez-faire economics*, which contends that less governmental intervention maximizes value. Conversely, Keynesian economics suggests a stronger role for government, particularly in times when the economy is strained. Both of these models assume rational, logical decision making. Newer models of economics question if human behavior is really altogether that logical and instead acknowledge the role of emotions in decision making. This approach is called *behavioral economics*. All of these orientations are useful to nurses. However, the economic conceptualization that is most useful to nursing care is *health economics*, yet another different approach that focuses on the unique aspects of health care markets.

Health Economics

Health economics is a relatively new discipline. It emerged as a distinct field following the 1963 publication of a manuscript by Nobel Prize–winning economist Kenneth Arrow titled *Uncertainty and the Welfare Economics of Medical Care*. Others built on Arrow's seminal work and furthered understanding of the ways health economics shapes health care.

WHY STUDY HEALTH ECONOMICS?

The models and theories of health economics—and the research they have spawned—are useful to nurses. Like a mirror or guidepost, understanding health economics helps the nurse make sense of the often convoluted, paradoxical, and invisible yet pervasive ways economics shapes the organization, financing, and delivery of health care. Moreover, many of the policy decisions at institutional, state, and federal levels relate to economic incentives and how the money flows through the system. Thus, to serve patients and help shape a world in which the holistic, patient-/family-/community-centric vision of the profession of nursing can become a reality, nurses need a confident command of economic terms and ideas and to be able to apply them in the practice setting.

Yet for many of us nurses, the interpersonal aspect of the nursing role—taking care of people and building relationships—is precisely what drew us to the nursing profession in the first place. Economics, with complex mathematical formulas, nuanced theories, and interfaces with systems-level finances, can seem far removed from the working knowledge, concerns, and everyday work life of the nurse. Nevertheless, the field of economics and the profession of nursing share key interests.

WHAT SORT OF THINGS DO ECONOMISTS THINK ABOUT?

Some of the most pressing issues of economics are also issues nurses face every day. For example (adapted from Kernick, 2003):

- *What do we do when there is more need than resources with which to meet this need?*
- *From what perspective should these competing demands be viewed: that of individuals, society at large, businesses, or health professionals? Or is there a way that these can be considered simultaneously?*
- *What is value, and how do we maximize it?*
- *What is the influence of health care on health?*

This latter question is of particular importance to nurses as well as society at large, as it relates to *social determinants of health* such as educational level and socioeconomic class.

SOCIAL DETERMINANTS OF HEALTH

Although nearly 18 cents of every dollar spent in the United States goes to health care, health care contributes only marginally to health. As illustrated in Figure 1.1, there is a substantial misalignment between where the United States spends its health care dollar and what impacts health. Although medical care receives nearly 90% of national health expenditures, this care contributes only roughly 10% to health status. Conversely, healthy behaviors contribute roughly 50% but received a mere 4% of national health expenditures (Network for Excellence in Health Innovation, 2012). The best overall predictors of health status are factors such as socioeconomic class and educational attainment. So, in the aggregate, the most healthy among us are educated Americans in good jobs who live in safe neighborhoods. This creates a paradoxical tension; when more public and private money is put into health care, there are fewer resources available for job creation and education, which in turn, means a whole population may have fewer opportunities for the education, employment, and a lifestyle that is associated with better health. Thus, how money is distributed ultimately impacts the health of a population through social determinants of health (see Box 1.1 for the World Health Organization definition of *social determinants of health*). Health economics concerns itself with these issues because it considers and analyzes the manner in which scarce resources are allocated, for example, in light of alternative ways to allocate resources that impact determinants. It also considers how resource allocation impacts human behavior.

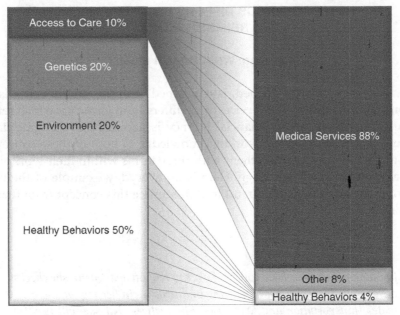

Figure 1.1
Spending for health determinants and health expenditures.
Adapted from Network for Excellence in Health Innovation (2012).

Box 1.1
What Are Social Determinants of Health?

The World Health Organization defines social determinants of health as follows:

Social determinants of health are the conditions in which people are born, grow, live, work, and age. These circumstances are shaped by the distribution of money, power and resources at global, national, and local levels. The social determinants of health are mostly responsible for health inequities—the unfair and unavoidable differences in health status seen within and between countries.

Source: World Health Organization (WHO, n.d.)

HOW ECONOMICS DIFFERS FROM FINANCING
AND REIMBURSEMENT

Financing: What Does it Mean?

Thus, *economics*, broadly defined, is concerned with the production, distribution, and consumption of services, and differs from *financing*, which refers to the obtaining of funds. Financial literacy is necessary to navigate daily life, and most nurses have a working knowledge of both of these concepts, despite not having identified them with these terms within their workplace or their professional knowledge. Here is an everyday example of the concept of financing. Please be careful to differentiate this concept from that of economics.

Justine has just completed college. Eager to rent an apartment, she checks the average monthly cost of housing and utilities in her region and estimates transportation and food costs. She realizes that she will need to clear at least $4,000/month if she lives alone, but with three roommates, that figure drops to $1,000/month. Justine decides that the latter is more feasible; she will need to find a way to finance $1,000/month.

As this general example illustrates, financing refers to how the resource comes to what is often called *the agent*—Justine in this example. In health care, the parallel to the agent to whom the resources are gathered is the *payer*, a concept that will be discussed shortly. Justine may have several options for financing her costs. She may find a job—certainly something most parents wish! She may instead ask for her parents to finance all or part of her monthly expenses. Or perhaps she is an heiress and can live off the interest of a trust fund. In any case, her expenses must first be financed. Note also that financing refers to how the money is obtained, but not what it is used for.

HOW IS HEALTH CARE FINANCED IN THE UNITED STATES?

The U.S. health care system also has several different mechanisms by which funds for health services are obtained. These U.S. health financing options include *out-of-pocket* money at the point of service from those who use health

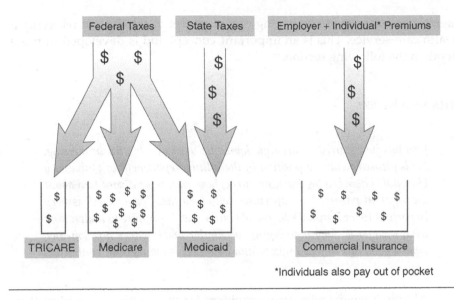

Figure 1.2
Financing of health care in the United States.

care, *taxes,* and *insurance premiums* (see Figure 1.2). Each of these is discussed in greater detail, but for now it is important to simply distinguish the difference between health financing and health economics; health economics is a broad term that refers to overarching questions about the allocation of scarce resources, whereas financing is a narrower term that relates to how the money for services is generated in the first place.

Reimbursement: How Are Providers of Health Care Paid?

These two concepts, economics and financing, differ still from another key concept, *reimbursement*. Reimbursement refers to the money paid to providers of care for services delivered and is discussed later in this chapter as well as throughout this text. Financing refers to how the financial resources (money) for health services are raised, and reimbursement refers to what and how providers are paid for providing those services. You can think about this as money going into a bucket (financing) and money later being poured back out to pay for services used (reimbursement). Those providing reimbursement, that is, paying providers for the delivery of health services, are aptly called *payers*. As used in health care, the term payers includes *commercial insurance companies* and state and federal governments, termed *governmental payers,* but not individuals paying out of pocket at the time of receiving a health care service. This is an important concept and is developed in more depth in the following section.

WHAT IS A PAYER?

Joey has just started a part-time job as he works on his BS in nursing. He is pleased to have a position in the billing department of University Hospital. There is a big learning curve, however, as he is confused about the different payers. The supervisor tells Joey that "payer mix" is very important to the hospital's financial status. Just beginning to understand what a payer is, Joey now begins to wonder what "payer mix" means, what a good mix or a bad mix is, and how that is managed or controlled.

Although payers reimburse providers for the health care services they provide, the process is different than for other goods and services because the payer is an intermediary between the user of the services—the patient—and the provider of the service, such as the doctor, hospital, nurse practitioner, or home health agency. Although nurses provide services, typically the term *provider* references those who are reimbursed by a payer, such as doctors and hospitals. This rather odd situation is largely the result of the historical evolution of employer-based health insurance and is detailed in Chapter 2.

PAYER MIX

Payer mix refers to the combination of different payers any one provider may be reimbursed by and the proportion of each. Different financing mechanisms have funds bucketed into different payment vehicles, that is, different payers. These can be considered *insurers,* so let us look more carefully at what the term insurance coverage really means.

Insurance Coverage

COMMERCIAL INSURANCE

Commercial insurance is insurance that an individual or business can purchase. Common examples include state-level programs like Blue Cross and

Blue Shield and national companies like Aetna, to mention just two. In the United States, these commercial insurance companies can be *nonprofit* or *for profit*; for-profit companies have the expressed mission of returning financial dividends to stockholders in the company. Nonprofit companies also intend to make a profit, but these must be retained by the organization to support self-preservation, growth, or new initiatives. In the case of a nonprofit company, that extra revenue is termed a *surplus* rather than a profit. Unlike for-profit companies, nonprofit companies do not have shareholders.

GOVERNMENTAL OR TAX-FUNDED INSURANCE COVERAGE

Medicare and Medicaid are tax-funded insurance coverage programs. They are federal programs, but with many differences. Medicare is overseen at a national level, meaning states have little say in how Medicare operates within the state. Medicaid is a federal program administered at a state level. Both have specific inclusion criteria. Medicare is a system of insurance coverage for those older than 65, whereas Medicaid is a program for poor and some disabled individuals. Medicare is finance via a federal payroll tax, whereas Medicaid is a mix of state and federal taxes. Together, Medicare, Medicaid, and the Children's Health Insurance Program (CHIPS) represented 22% of the federal budget, or $772 billion, in 2012. Nearly two-thirds of this was Medicare (Centers on Budget and Policy Priorities, 2014). Given these percentages, it is easy to see that our government is heavily involved in (a) financing health care and (b) playing a major role as payer. Thus, the next time you hear someone say "Government has no place in health care," you can sagely respond, knowing that our government is deeply involved in U.S. health care as a financier through taxes and as a payer through Medicare, Medicaid, CHIPS, and TRICARE, the program for military dependents and military members using health care services not available through other means.

PAYER MIX AND COST SHIFTING

Each of these payers reimburses providers at different levels. Medicare theoretically reimburses *at cost*, whereas Medicaid reimburses below the cost of service provision. The numbers and proportions of individuals on Medicaid vary from state to state. This is because states have jurisdiction over the level of poverty at which an individual is eligible for Medicaid coverage. One state may start to cover individuals at 133% of poverty, for example, meaning that according to *Federal Poverty Level (FPL) Guidelines*, the person would need to make $1,293 or less to be eligible for Medicaid. Another state may be more generous, allowing a person to make up to 300% of the FPL, or up to $2,918,[1] and still be eligible for Medicaid benefits. This difference impacts the proportion of Medicaid-supported patients the delivery setting will see and treat. This proportion matters: No organization can consistently lose money, pay its employees (including nurses), and ultimately stay in business. If Medicare is a primary payer for a large number of patients in a given clinic, for example, that clinic may need to seek and treat a larger number of patients with commercial insurance, which pays at a higher rate than Medicaid *and* Medicare for the same services, and thus balance the clinic budget. It is also the reason payer mix is so important to any provider. A setting with more commercially insured patients and fewer Medicaid-insured patients will have a more robust financial situation than one with the obverse situation. This phenomenon of higher reimbursement from commercial insurance to offset the lower reimbursement from Medicare and Medicaid has the curious name of *cost shifting*, even though it is not cost that it shifts but charges. Understanding cost shifting can be very difficult for the lay public because it seems illogical that one payer would reimburse so differently than another for the exact same service. Because understanding cost shifting is so important to understanding commercial insurance rate hikes, it is discussed in more detail shortly. First, however, it is important to take a deeper dive into insurance and how it works.

Insurance or the Well Carry the Sick

Oscar is furious. He was hoping for a big raise this year, and things seemed on track. Now this! Big Company Human Resources just issued an announcement that the cost of health insurance is going up more than expected next year. Although a 2% across-the-board salary increase and a 3% merit pool had been anticipated, the increasing cost of commercial health insurance is going to eat away most of that 5% pool. Some employees may even see a resulting decrease in their take-home pay. Seething, Oscar mutters, "Those insurance companies are just so greedy."

Tim is the CEO of Statewide Insurance Company. Reviewing the financials for the past year, he notes that there had been a dramatic increase in the use of health care by the employees in Big Company. Not only were more employees using health care, they were using very expensive health care. "I wonder if the employees realize that their use of health care in the previous year is a contributing factor to the rate hike this year."

Perhaps because insurance costs are always on the rise, insurance companies often are on the receiving end of a great deal of negative public attention. Yet, in nonprofit insurance companies ("nonprofit" meaning those that are not designed to make profits to return to company shareholders), insurance premiums—the amount members pay each month to be insured—reflect health care use by the members, overhead to manage associated administrative costs, and a solvency pool or sort of safety net savings account in case there is an unexpectedly high number of claims. The latter are termed *reserves*.

Thus, insurance is a form of financial *risk sharing*, in which funds are redistributed from those who are not using health services to those who are (see Figure 1.3). In health care, the *well carry the sick*, with those who use

Figure 1.3
How insurance works.

few services financially covering much of the cost of services for those who use many. Typically, an individual does not know when or if he or she will need health services, and it is therefore an uncertain financial risk. By design, insurance spreads the financial risk out among the members of the insurance group.

A SIMPLE EXAMPLE TO ILLUSTRATE HOW INSURANCE WORKS

To illustrate, imagine two scenarios. In the first, you are uninsured. You are in a small accident, and the cost of your care is $1,000. You are responsible to pay the full $1,000 to those who treated you. These providers of health care may be hospitals, physicians, nurse practitioners, or others, such as physical therapists. In the second scenario, you again have an accident resulting in a $1,000 charge, but this time you are in an insurance group of 1,000 people. Now the risk is shared by everyone, and hypothetically each person's contribution to your care is a mere one dollar. Health insurance, although a bit more complicated, works exactly like this in concept, except that the payment from each member of the group does not happen individually at the time of your accident. Instead, it happens in the form of a monthly *premium*, with the term premium referring to the amount each member pays to the insurance company each month. The insurance company then, in turn, doles out reimbursement for services to providers. If there is a great deal of use of health care services, or a few members are receiving a great deal of very high cost services, the insurance premium for the whole group will go up the next year. The insurance company uses the cost experience of the group to determine the likely amount of money needed in the next year. In short, insurance premiums mirror the underlying cost of care for individuals within the group insurance plan.

WHAT FACTORS IMPACT COST WITHIN A RISK-SHARING ARRANGEMENT?

The size and nature of the group that is sharing risk matters. In a large group, there are simply more people among whom risk may be spread. Again, by way of illustration, imagine a hypothetical group in which there were only three people. In this small group, there are not many people among whom the costs of care can be spread. Therefore, in general, a larger insurance group, such as employers with many workers, will be able to have lower monthly premiums, more covered services, or both because there are more people to spread out this uncertain risk.

The health status, age, and other aspects of members of the pool also impact the cost of care for individuals in the insurance group and so ultimately also impact the cost of their insurance premiums. This concept is familiar. Here are examples from automobile insurance:

> Moira is glad to be alive! Driving through a rural area of Kentucky, her car suddenly skidded off the road into a tree. Although she was fine, her car was totaled. Three days later, although still relieved that she escaped unharmed, she ponders: "I wonder how much my insurance rates will go up."

This is an example of what is called *experience rating*, where your individual history directly impacts the cost of your insurance. It can also impact you because you are a member of a high-risk group.

> Moira's 15-year-old son, Josh, has just received his driver's permit. She is well aware that her insurance premium will go up when she puts Josh on her car insurance policy. Novice drivers have more accidents and, overall, young men have more accidents than young women. Josh, no matter how responsible he is, fits the profile of these high-risk, high-cost insurees. Moira knows that insuring Josh will bring a dramatic increase in her monthly premiums.

Experience rating is one approach to risk appraisal. The second is *community rating*. In experience rating, ill *individuals* pay higher premiums than well individuals. In community rating, ill *groups* pay higher premiums than well groups. Health insurance plans using experience rating will charge higher insurance costs for older, sicker individuals than for individuals who are younger and well. Similarly, individuals who are in high-risk occupations would have higher premiums. Unlike experience rating, community rating redistributes charges evenly throughout the group insured. Community rating charges all individuals in the same group the same premium cost, regardless of their age, gender, occupation, or other factors that impact health. Thus, cost increases for an individual reflect the group experience over the previous year.

Which is better: experience rating or community rating? Although on the surface it may seem logical that those who are well have less expensive premiums than those who are not, experience rating results in more expensive premiums for those who most need health care. Recall that the foundational premise of health care insurance is that it redistributes funds by human need; community rating does this more consistently than experience rating (Bodenheimer & Grumbach, 2012). Community rating evens out the insurance charges throughout the group, meaning that some well people will have higher costs than they would in experience rating, as they are carrying the cost of others. At some point, however, it likely will be their turn, and others will carry the cost of their care. Some states have passed laws to assure that only community rating or modified community rating will be allowed within the state.

INSURANCE INDUSTRY CHANGES SINCE THE PASSAGE OF THE ACA

Of course, people prefer lower monthly premiums, so those insurance policies with lower premiums have a competitive advantage over those with higher premiums. One way a group's health care insurance premiums can be kept low is to exclude those with known health conditions from the insurance pool. Prior to the passage of the ACA of 2010, sometimes referred to as Obamacare, two strategies of limiting cost of an insurance product were allowed. These were (a) *preexisting health condition exclusions*, meaning that if individuals have a health condition when they apply for insurance and that condition is judged to make them liable to need extensive and/or expensive health care, they may be excluded from an insurance group; and (b) limits on how much will be paid over a lifetime, called *lifetime caps*, which means there is a limit on the total amount one can receive for one's health care. This can pose a real problem if a person is suddenly faced with a catastrophe with ongoing health consequences or if he or she has chronic conditions and reaches the cap. Although these strategies can keep a group's insurance premium lower, it denies health insurance to those in greatest need of care, which violates the very rationale for insurance in the first place.

What the ACA Requires

The ACA has addressed these and other elements of the way health insurance has worked in the United States. This law requires insurance companies to remove the lifetime caps on the amount that can be paid for the care of an individual. It also ends the provisions that allowed insurance companies to deny insurance to an individual based on a preexisting health condition. This opens the opportunity for those previously uninsurable to be able to access health insurance. The ACA also allows adult children to stay on their parent's health insurance policy up to the age of 26, even when they are not dependents or in college. These provisions increase access to health insurance, but they do not decrease the overall cost.

HOW ELSE DOES HEALTH REFORM IMPACT FINANCIAL ACCESS TO HEALTH CARE?

The ACA of 2010 is a *national health insurance program* that requires all citizens to be covered by one or a combination of the forms of insurance coverage listed in Table 1.1 and thus is a *hybrid financing model* with multiple payers. Individuals who are not covered by Medicare or Medicaid are required to have commercial insurance. This requirement is termed a *mandate*. There are two types of mandates in the ACA, *employer mandates* and *individual mandates*.

Employer Mandates
Employers with more than 50 employees will be required to provide health care coverage for their employees or face a financial penalty. Originally planned to take effect in 2014, this part of the law was delayed until 2015 to allow employers more time to comply because those companies that were not paying for employee insurance, or not paying enough, now face a *financing* challenge to meet the new requirement.

Table 1.1
U.S. Health Care Payers, by Financing Mechanism

Financing Mechanism	Entity	Payer
Federal payroll tax	Medicare	Federal government
Federal and state taxes	Medicaid	Federal program administered by state governments, within federal guidelines
Employees and employers	Private employer–based insurance	Private insurance companies (commercial insurance)
Individuals/families	Individually purchased insurance	Private insurance companies (commercial insurance)
Individuals/families	Individually purchased through health insurance exchanges	Private insurance companies (commercial insurance)

Individual Mandates

In addition to this employer mandate, that law includes an *individual mandate* under which an individual who does not have employer-based insurance, Medicare, or Medicaid is required to have insurance or, similar to the employer mandate, pay a penalty. The individual mandate survived a Supreme Court challenge to its constitutionality and remains the law of the land.

What About Individuals Who Cannot Afford to Comply With the Individual Mandate?

What about those who cannot afford to purchase health insurance? The ACA also has provisions for financial assistance to help those who cannot afford the cost of insurance. This form of financial assistance is called a *subsidy*. In addition, the law includes provisions that create the opportunity for individuals to better understand what they are buying when they purchase health insurance. To help individuals make the best choice for themselves, in terms of both cost and coverage, the law also includes the *health insurance marketplace*, typically referred to as *health care exchanges*. The exchange is actually a menu of options designed to enable individuals and small businesses to see what insurance packages are available and compare cost and other trade-offs. Despite the rocky rollout of the exchanges due to the complexities of the technological interfaces and demands, the overall concept behind the exchanges is very simple: comparison as a basis for choice.

WHAT DOES THE HEALTH CARE EXCHANGE DO?

Comparing health insurance plans can be confusing. Therefore, to be sure there are apples-to-apples comparisons, each plan must cover the same set of basic benefits. These basic, core benefits are termed *essential health benefits* (see Box 1.2). The essential health benefits also include some elements of prevention and screening that must be provided at no charge to the patient, meaning the financial disincentives to use these services have been removed (see Box 1.3). The definition of what services must be included is an important one; prior to this requirement, an individual may have purchased less expensive health insurance, only to find it was less expensive because it did not cover many services and left the person unexpectedly responsible for services he or she received.

What Is Different Among Plans in the Health Insurance Exchange?

What does differ among the options within the health care exchange is the balance between monthly premiums and associated *cost sharing*, that is, the

Box 1.2

Essential Health Benefits Required by the Affordable Care Act

Ambulatory patient services

Chronic disease management

Emergency services

Hospitalizations

Laboratory tests

Maternity and newborn care

Mental health and substance use disorder services, including behavioral health treatment (this includes counseling and psychotherapy)

Pediatric services

Prescription drugs

Preventive services (see Box 1.3)

Rehabilitative services and devices

Source: HealthCare.gov (n.d.).

Box 1.3

Affordable Care Act–Required Preventative Services

Abdominal aortic aneurysm one-time screening for men of specified ages who have ever smoked

Alcohol misuse screening and counseling

Aspirin use to prevent cardiovascular disease for men and women of certain ages

Blood pressure screening for all adults

Cholesterol screening for adults of certain ages or at higher risk

Colorectal cancer screening for adults over 50

Depression screening for adults

Diabetes (type 2) screening for adults with high blood pressure

Diet counseling for adults at higher risk for chronic disease

HIV screening for everyone ages 15 to 65, and other ages at increased risk

Immunization vaccines for adults—doses, recommended ages, and recommended populations vary

Source: HealthCare.gov (n.d.).

amount that a person enrolled in that plan would pay out of pocket. Lower monthly premium plans will have higher patient cost sharing at the time the patient uses health care services. Because of their name—*Bronze, Silver, Gold, and Platinum*—the different categories of essential health benefit plans within the exchange are sometime termed *metals*. These metals differ not in what services are covered, but rather in how individuals choose to balance the cost. Platinum, for example, has the highest monthly premium, but the lowest out-of-pocket expense when using services. Bronze has the lowest monthly premium of the metals, but the highest out-of-pocket expenses when using health services. There is even a term for the average proportion of health care that is paid for by the individual out of pocket. This term, *actuarial value*, is set at roughly 60%, 70%, 80%, and 90%, for bronze, silver, gold, and platinum, respectively. So, for example, a bronze plan pays for 60% of services used; platinum pays for 90%.

So, why would anyone choose a bronze plan? The trade-off is in the ongoing cost of the monthly premium, which is lowest in the bronze plan. Young persons who are betting they will not need health services may choose a bronze plan with the lowest monthly premiums, seeing that as a better value than paying higher monthly insurance premiums for care they do not expect to use. Conversely, persons with any chronic conditions may choose to pay more each month, the platinum plan, for example, because they know they use a lot of health care services and want the reassurance that 90% will be covered, especially if that is 90% of a very large health care bill. The subsidies—the difference between what a person's expected contribution to insurance is and what he or she actually pays—are, by law, benchmarked to the silver.

Are There Other Low-Cost Plans in the Exchange?
There is one more category of health insurance plans in the exchanges required by the ACA. These are termed *catastrophic plans*. These plans also cover the essential health benefits to some degree, but differ from the bronze plans in that catastrophic plans do not cover 60% of the health care costs. Instead, they cover three primary care visits and certain preventative services and only cover additional services after the deductible of $6,350 for an individual plan or $12,700 for a family and thus typically would have an actuarial value of less than 60%. Federally funded tax credits and subsidies are not available for individuals covered by catastrophic plans, and participation is limited to those under 30 or those who cannot find coverage for less than 8% of their income.

WHERE CAN A NURSE DIRECT A PATIENT WHO ASKS QUESTIONS ABOUT HOW TO NAVIGATE THE COMPLEX TERRAIN OF HEALTH INSURANCE?

Nurses are well-trusted health professionals, and patient education across a range of issues is a core competency of nurses. That said, the decision of which plan to choose can have enormous consequences for a family; nurses who are asked advice on health insurance should be prepared with the general knowledge heretofore described, but may—understandably and appropriately—still feel at a loss to provide specific direction. Fortunately, *navigators* have been trained to help people find their way through the health insurance exchange. Nurses can feel confident about referring patients who ask questions about the exchange to these trained navigators. Take a moment to determine where navigators can be found in your region. Some states are also attempting to create user-friendly exchange websites in which individuals can include personal information like income to readily determine which plan would offer them the greatest financial or other advantage, including subsidies or tax credits. Unfortunately, simple-to-use sites can be complex to build, and at the time of this writing, some states are struggling to make their sites fully operational. Take a moment to review the health insurance exchange website in your state.

The ACA and Out-of-Pocket Maximums

For individuals choosing the bronze or silver plan or catastrophic coverage, the decision to keep money in their pocket each month may also be reinforced by another provision of the ACA that sets limits on the total amount of health care costs an individual or family will pay each year. This is termed *out-of-pocket maximum* or *out-of-pocket limits*, set at no more than $6,350 for individuals and $12,700 for a family (HealthCare.gov, 2014). Note that there were no out-of-pocket limits prior to the ACA, and—although for many families this is still a lot of money—a single hospitalization could far exceed this amount and would have fallen to the underinsured or uninsured family to pay prior to the required coverage in the ACA or would have been provided at a financial loss to the hospital as *charity care* or *bad debt*.

CONCLUSION

Health economics considers issues of value and efficiency, whereas financing considers how funds are gathered. One mechanism by which health care is financed is health insurance, and the ACA has built on the existing employer-based insurance model to ensure insurance coverage for all Americans. There are many other provisions in the ACA. Yet, to move forward and understand the significance of each of these and what they mean to nurses and their patients, a firm understanding of the evolution of the U.S. health system is essential. As shown by the contrast between Will and Mary Jane in the opening scenarios, contemporary nurses face a complicated world. Many of the troubling elements of the current health care system are the result of the unintended consequences of the solutions adopted to address health system shortcomings. It is like an economic whack-a-mole game: One problem solved immediately creates another unsolved one. These unintended consequences are a driver of the evolution of the health care system to its present form. This is the focus of Chapter 2.

Thought Questions

1. What is health economics? How is it similar to and different from other branches of economics? How does it differ from health financing?

2. Who pays for health care in the United States? How?

3. What is the role of government in the financing of U.S. health care?

4. What elements of health care financing existed before the Affordable Care Act? What elements are new?

5. What is the best way to finance health care? Why?

6. What are the pros and cons of risk-rated insurance and community-rated insurance? Which is better and why?

7. Define the following key terms:

Actuarial value	Classic free market
Affordable Care Act of 2010	Commercial insurance
Behavioral economics	Community rating
Catastrophic insurance	Cost sharing

Employer mandates

Experience rating

Governmental payers

Health economics

Health care financing

Health insurance marketplace

Individual mandates

Keynesian economics

Laissez-faire economics

Lifetime caps

Metal levels

Payer

Payer mix

Preexisting health condition

Premium

Profit

Reimbursement

Reserves

Risk sharing

Social determinants of health

Surplus

Exercises

1. You are asked to present to Nursing Grand Rounds. The organizers share that nurses seem to be confused about insurance-related aspects of the Affordable Care Act of 2010. Develop your talk to address these concerns.

2. Develop a short presentation to describe the health insurance exchange in your state.

Quiz

TRUE OR FALSE

1. In health care, financing and reimbursement refer to the same thing.

2. Health economics is a distinct branch in the field of economics.

3. The best overall predictor of health status of a population is access to health care.

4. Commercial insurance companies in the United States are always nonprofit organizations.

5. There is no difference in the amount of reimbursement providers receive from different payers.

6. In *experience rating*, insurance companies charge ill individuals more for health insurance than well individuals.

7. In health care, the *health insurance marketplace* and the *health care exchange* refer to the same thing.

8. The Affordable Care Act of 2010 allows individuals to stay on their parent's health insurance until age 26, as long as they are dependents listed on a tax return or in college.

9. The Affordable Care Act of 2010 is sometimes called *Obamacare*.

10. The term for the minimal health benefits required by the Affordable Care Act is *essential health benefits*.

MULTIPLE CHOICE

11. In the United States, health care is financed via
    A. Taxes
    B. Insurance premiums
    C. Patients, as an out-of-pocket expense
    D. All of the above

12. Medicare
    A. Is a publicly financed health care coverage for most Americans 65 years and over
    B. Is financed through a combination of state and federal taxes
    C. Both A and B
    D. Neither A nor B

13. One insurance-related element of the Affordable Care Act of 2010 is
    A. The elimination of lifetime caps, the total amount an insurance company would pay any one individual for health care–related expenses
    B. Strengthening the preexisting exclusion clauses in health insurance, making it more difficult for individuals to obtain insurance
    C. Both A and B
    D. Neither A nor B

14. The health care financing plan of the Affordable Care Act includes
    A. Individual mandates
    B. Employer mandates
    C. Both A and B
    D. Neither A nor B

15. The term *actuarial value*
    A. Refers to the clinical value of a particular health care service or treatment
    B. Is eliminated in community-rated insurance
    C. Both A and B
    D. Neither A nor B

16. Individuals who are specially trained to help others understand health care insurance options in the health insurance exchange are called
    A. Brokers
    B. Navigators
    C. Actuaries
    D. Subsidizers

17. The term *payer mix* refers to the proportion of reimbursement a provider receives from commercial insurance, Medicare, and Medicaid. Payer mix is important because
    A. Organizations are reimbursed by Medicare at higher rates than the other payers
    B. It provides a financial incentive for providers to treat patients who are on Medicaid
    C. Both A and B
    D. Neither A nor B

18. The Affordable Care Act
    A. Sets what is termed *out-of-pocket limits* for individuals and families, limiting the total amount any one person or family would pay in health care costs in any one year
    B. Eliminates the cost shift
    C. Both A and B
    D. Neither A nor B

NOTE

1. 2014 FPL Guidelines for a family size of one.

REFERENCES

Arrow, K. (1963). Uncertainty and the welfare economics of medical care. *The American Economic Review, 53*(5), 941–973.

Bodenheimer, T., & Grumbach, K. (2012). *Understanding health policy: A clinical approach.* New York, NY: McGraw Hill/Lang.

Centers on Budget and Policy Priorities. (2014, March 31). *Issues for Congress' lame duck session.* Retrieved June 14, 2014, from http://www.cbpp.org

HealthCare.gov (2014). *Glossary.* Retrieved July 2, 2014, from http://www.healthcare.gov/glossary

HealthCare.gov (n.d.). *What marketplace health plans cover.* Retrieved from https://www.healthcare.gov/what-does-marketplace-health-insurance-cover

Kernick, D. (2003). Introduction to health economics for the medical practitioner. *Postgraduate Medical Journal, 79,* 147–150.

Network for Excellence in Health Innovation. (2012). *The Boston paradox: Lots of health care, not enough health care.* Cambridge, MA: Author.

World Health Organization. (n.d.). *What are social determinants of health?* Retrieved July 26, 2014, from http://www.who.int/topics/social_determinants/en

A STORY OF UNINTENDED CONSEQUENCES: HOW ECONOMIC AND POLICY SOLUTIONS CREATE NEW CHALLENGES

CHAPTER 2 DETAILS the evolution of the U.S. employer-based fee-for-service system and the rise of tax-funded financing via Medicare and Medicaid. Following completion of this chapter, you will be able to

- Detail the historic context that gave rise to contemporary health care financing mechanisms and the biomedical orientation to care
- Discuss early payment reform models such as prospective payment and health maintenance organizations
- Describe the financing approach of the Affordable Care Act (ACA)

Carolyn is excited to visit her great-grandfather in the assisted living facility. Born in 1916, he is full of tales of the old West. Papa John, as Carolyn calls him, beams with pride when she shares that she has just graduated with her baccalaureate degree and is practicing as an RN. Thinking about health care, Papa John begins to muse on the flu epidemic of 1918. He shares that his older brother, Nick, nearly died of what Papa now thinks was diphtheria. The country doctor could do nothing for Nick, and finally, with Nick near death, his mother called on Florence, the village "wise woman." Florence crushed herbs to create a compound and, with a sheet of paper rolled to a cone, blew the compound into Nick's mouth. Later that night, Nick's fever broke, and by morning he was well. Papa shares that his mother always credited the village woman with saving her son's life. Carolyn, who just received her first paycheck, wonders about compensation for services rendered. "Papa," she asks, "did you pay Florence anything?" "Of course," Papa proudly responds. "Every fall we would give her a chicken!" Carolyn ponders the barter system and concludes that she and her classmates are very happy to be paid with money, not chickens.[1]

Shanice is a nurse practitioner in a primary care clinic in a major urban area. She is mostly satisfied with her job, but is hoping for a substantial raise in salary following her upcoming annual review. In preparation, she decides to talk to the clinic business manager about her salary hopes. The business manages firmly states that the availability of funds for a raise will depend on three factors: (1) The clinic's achievement of quality metrics for those patients within the pay-for-performance system; (2) rates negotiated with the insurance company for those patients in the independent provider arrangement; and (3) changing the ratio of Medicaid to private pay patients, so that the clinic sees fewer Medicaid patients and more private pay patients. "Is it really this complicated," Shanice wonders, "or is the business manager just trying to put me off?"

Most U.S. nurses have entered professional life at a time when employer-based insurance represented the most common private financing mechanism and fee-for-service the primary mechanism for reimbursing providers. Similarly, Medicaid and Medicare, also using fee-for-service reimbursement mechanisms, have been publicly funded fixtures in health care since 1965. Together, these predominant models seem "normal" or just how health care costs are managed. Thus, it is often a surprise to discover that this commonplace situation is almost a fluke of history, studded with unintended consequences and fixes to those consequences with yet new unintended consequences.

As Carolyn learned from her great-grandfather, health care had a very different profile in the early 1900s. Infections and injuries were common causes of death, and little—other than easing suffering and hoping for the best—could be done to help those in need. Like the wise woman serving Papa John's brother, providers of care were often not paid at all or were compensated within some sort of barter system. Imagine, for a moment, if in your practice as an RN, you were compensated with what people had to give you, if they had something to give you, when they could, like the yearly chicken that Florence received.

THE INFLUENCE OF THE FLEXNER REPORT

Several forces of history changed the course of U.S. health care from the world described in the opening vignette and set the stage for the medical industrial complex it is today. The first of these is the Flexner report, which reformed medical education.

In the early 1900s, education for physicians was loosely organized. There were many for-profit schools, with no uniform standards for students' education and training. At the urging of the American Medical Association and in response to concerns about the quality and consistency of care, the Carnegie Foundation hired Abraham Flexner, an educational reformer, to study medical education in the United States and Canada. Flexner concluded that the problems in medical education resulted from having too many schools preparing physicians and the lack of uniformity in that education. Flexner was influenced by the "hyper-rational world of German medicine" (Duffy, 2011, p. 276) and by the biomedical model he saw at Johns Hopkins and their curricular approach that focused on laboratory sciences and research. As Duffy notes, Flexner rated schools in comparison to Johns Hopkins as follows:

> Schools were assigned to one of three categories on the basis of his evaluation: A first group consisted of those that compared favorably with Hopkins; a second tier was comprised of those schools considered substandard but which could be salvaged by supplying financial assistance to correct the deficiencies; and a third group was rated of such poor quality that closure was indicated. The latter was the fate of one-third of American medical schools in the aftermath of the report. (p. 272)

Schools with less financial resources and less developed science departments had a difficult time meeting the criteria, and many of these served people of color and women. Barkin, Fuentes-Afflick, Brosco, and Tuchman (2010) note that the Flexner criteria for medical education forced the closure of most of the schools serving black and female medical students, and opportunities for women and students of color evaporated; in the years following the Flexner report, there was an increase in both the numbers and proportions of white male medical students and a decrease in students with other salient identity markers, with a near elimination of women from the physician workforce between the years 1920 and 1970. Medical education following the Johns Hopkins model also became longer and more expensive (Harley, 2006). The review by Prislin, Saultz, and Geyman (2010) of unintended consequences of the Flexner report notes that the socioeconomic schism in admission to medical school continues to this day, given that 75% of U.S. medical students are from the two upper-income quintiles, that is, upper class or upper middle class. These authors also note that the Flexner Report spurred physician specialization rather than the primary care orientation common in other countries that have high-performing, less expensive health care systems. Moreover, Flexner's model was focused on a biological and physiological orientation, creating a shift away from and eventual closure of preparation programs for what we now call "complementary and alternative medicine"–oriented hospitals, colleges, and teaching programs. Indeed, following the Flexner Report, 80% of the programs in homeopathy, naturopathy, eclectic therapy, physical theory, osteopathy, and chiropractic closed (Stahnisch & Verhoef, 2012). Notably, today, such orientations are termed "complementary" or "alternative" in contrast to what we now see as "traditional" care, which is care within the Flexner model. But, as the opening scenario illustrated, there was no complementary, alternative, or standard medical care at the time. There were only sick individuals and those who wanted to treat them using the skills and information of their training. Thinking back to Carolyn's great-grandfather, it appears that Florence may have been more successful in treating Nick than the medical doctor was, and we do not know how either of them was trained. After the Flexner report, medical education became less diverse and more controlled, as it transitioned from a for-profit apprenticeship model to one that is university based with carefully selected students (Prislin, Saultz, & Geyman, 2010). On the flip side, it excluded many and created a scientific orientation that Duffy concludes was not balanced by similar excellence in caring.

What About Nurses?

Physicians also carved out a broad and exclusive scope of practice for themselves, with echoes to the present day with, for example, the American

Medical Association's opposition to expanded nursing scope of practice. Nurses, if educated at all, were trained in hospitals with entry-level responsibilities similar to that of a maid. To this day, hospitals bundle nurses' professional work into room charges. Consider Abigale's story, a young woman preparing as a nurse:

> *1915. Abigale, orphaned at age 13, has just completed her nursing training at Saint Alexius Hospital. The founding sisters could be tough, but she learned a great deal. "With any luck at all," Abigale muses, "I'll get a job working for a nice, wealthy family. Maybe they will even have a room for me!"*

After graduation, most nurses worked as private duty nurses at minimal wages, even though only families with resources could afford to hire a nurse in the first place. Nursing education did not bring social status or financial independence. Thus, the changes shaped by the Flexner Report set the stage for medicine, but not nursing, to be a regulated, organized, well-compensated profession. The Flexner Report set in motion a cascade of effects that continues to influence health and health care over one hundred years later, an example of the power of policy to create lasting change.

EARLY HOSPITALS

Just as the profession of medicine of 100 years ago was very different from the one of today, so too were the hospitals. Sultz and Young (2011) note: "Hospitals in early America served quite different purposes from those of today. They were founded to shelter older adults, the dying, orphans, and vagrants, and to protect the inhabitants of a community from the contagiously sick and the dangerously insane" (p. 70). Hospitals were dirty, overcrowded, and contaminated, and those with other options would not choose hospital care over the care that could be provided in their own homes. Over time, however, religious orders saw the opportunities to serve vulnerable individuals, and religious nursing groups played an important role in the development of hospitals (Sultz & Young, 2011). Some of these orders, for example, the Order of Saint Benedict, included "care of the sick" as a central tenet in their guiding *Rule of Saint Benedict* and organized elements of their monastic life around such care, including the establishment of hospitals.

The Introduction of Employer-Based Health Insurance

Nevertheless, despite some advances in hospital care, many potential patients remained uninterested in hospital service or were unable to pay for hospital services. As a result, many hospitals were not able to consistently attract patients. In response, Baylor University Hospital had a brilliant and, for the time, somewhat radical idea about how to attract "customers" in the form of patients capable of paying for care. In 1929, they began to offer 1,500 Dallas schoolteachers up to 21 days of hospital care for $6 a year per person. As the Great Depression intensified and people had even less money for anything at all, much less something like hospital care, hospital-centered prepaid insurance plans, requiring the use of a particular hospital, grew. In turn, these prepaid hospital plans became the basis of the American Hospital Association's establishment of Blue Cross, which differed in that they allowed patients a choice of hospitals. Initially opposed by physicians, the opportunity for guaranteed income became of interest to physician groups, as the Great Depression took effect, and people could not afford to see a doctor. The first Blue Shield plan was set up the by California Medical Association in 1939, and similar plans quickly spread across the nation. It is important to note that Blue Cross, established by the American Hospital Association, financially enabled and thus encouraged the use of hospital care, while Blue Shield financially enabled and thus encouraged the use of physician care, all within the biomedical model of care heralded by the Flexner Report. In retrospect, what is notable in these plans is the lack of incentives for quality, cost control, or appropriate utilization, because these organizations emerged to address a different problem: finding ways to ensure that hospitals and physicians were paid (Bodenheimer & Grumbach, 2012; Starr, 1982).

SOCIAL REFORM ADDRESSING UNINTENDED CONSEQUENCES OF EMPLOYER-BASED INSURANCE

The model of employer-based insurance that started with Dallas teachers grew rapidly because of another historical event: World War II. During World War II, employers were constrained by wage and price controls and so instead looked to *fringe benefits* as a strategy to recruit and retain workers. Employer-based health insurance is one such fringe benefit. Yet employer-based insurance has one dramatic unintended consequence: It leaves out those who are not employed! These include retired individuals, those with a disability or other challenges precluding work, those who are self-employed (like artists), and the partners or children of parents who are not working or do not have family health insurance. By the 1960s, the group most likely to be living in poverty was the elderly, with nearly three-fourths of U.S. elders living below the poverty line (DeLew, 2000).

In the social climate of the 1960s, it is not surprising that a sweeping corrective action was undertaken, reflecting testimony such as this:

> I am one of your old retired teachers that has been forgotten. I am 80 years old and for 10 years I have been living on a bare nothing, two meals a day, one egg, a soup, because I want to be independent....And I worked so hard that I have pernicious anemia, $9.95 for a little bottle of liquid for shots, wholesale, I couldn't pay for it. (Stevens, as cited in DeLew, 2000, p. 76)

As corrective action, Medicare, a publicly funded fee-for-service insurance overseen by the federal government for those older than 65, was established in 1965. Also established in 1965 was Medicaid, a publicly funded fee-for-service federal program administrated by states for low income individuals families with children, and most disabled and blind individuals under 65. At the time, President Lyndon Johnson's "Great Society" was a social reform movement that aimed to eliminate poverty. It was within this social milieu that Medicare and Medicaid were signed into law on July 30, 1965, as amendments to the Social Security Act, attempting to correct the gaps that emerged under employment-based insurance models. Notably, President Franklin D. Roosevelt had decided not to include health insurance in the original Social Security Act because of fierce opposition from physicians. Roosevelt feared that such inclusion would mean the demise of the entire Social Security program he was trying to establish. President Johnson presented the first two Medicare cards to former President Truman and Mrs. Truman and at the ceremony noted: "We marvel not simply at the passage of this bill, but what we marvel at is that it took so many years to pass" (Harris, as cited in DeLew, p. 75). In summary, Medicare, now a staple of the American health care system, was a hard-won, long-in-the-making reform.

Public Funding Fuels Health Industry Growth

Public financing for those older than 65, the poor, and those whose disabilities precluded employment heralded a new era in the American health care system. For the first time, there was a guaranteed revenue stream to treat those who, in aggregate, were guaranteed to be ill or seek health care services. Before the advent of these health-financing approaches, these individuals had a substantial incentive to avoid seeking treatment: They were solely responsible for paying for those services. Medicare and Medicaid removed the financial disincentives for these large groups of people in the society—the elderly, the poor, and the disabled—to seek treatment. In the same vein, under fee-for-service reimbursement, physicians and hospitals had no financial disincentive to limit treatment, both necessary and unnecessary. Thus fueled, the health care industry began its explosive growth. Physician income, which prior to 1965 tracked the annual inflation growth rate, skyrocketed. The money in the system also fueled the growth of specialty services and progressively more technologically enhanced services in hospitals (e.g., intensive care units and cardiac monitoring), and with it, new roles for nurses as well as the growth of roles for other providers. These emerging roles, then called "allied health" roles—presumably because they were "allied" with medicine and its social, political, and financial power—became *unbundled* from other services. In the early 1970s, for example, nurses debrided wounds and provided complex ambulation for hospitalized patients. These services were bundled in room charge fees, much like the maid services that marked nursing's early hospital history. Soon, however, such services became to be provided by physical therapists, for an additional charge or "fee-for-service." These professions then also had the financial fuel to grow their services, both in complexity and volume. In summary, when fully insured, patients had little incentive to limit the different services they sought and received; hospital, specialty services, and "allied health" grew, and some services once provided by nurses were unbundled from nursing care and provided by other providers. Nursing specialization also grew, in response to clinical realities and financial opportunities.

However, one person's income or revenue stream is another's expense. Commercial insurance, as noted in the first chapter, exists to spread financial risk, and the well carry the sick financially, with costs of care spread through the group. Similarly, the costs of care for those in publicly funded insurance such as Medicare and Medicaid are spread through society through taxes (review Figure 1.3 for an illustration of how insurance works). This means that even though individuals using the services may not feel the immediate financial impact of their use of services, in aggregate, the use of health care by individuals in the group uses tax dollars. In turn, less tax money remains for other goods and services, for example, public funding of higher education to keep college tuition affordable. Similarly, although employer-based insurance seems to be "paid for by my employer," it is actually a portion of the total compensation package the employee receives. Any increase in the use of health services results in increased insurance costs, which are borne by the employee as a reduction in possible wage increases or expanded fringe benefits. Regardless of the source of the resources, taken as a whole, the availability of private insurance complemented by Medicare and Medicaid all within a fee-for-service system dramatically drove up the use of medical services. The use of the term "medical" services rather than "health" care here is intentional. Recall the orientation of the Flexner Report and its influence on medical education; Blue Shield was a physician's organization, and the physicians were uniformly educated within the biological model of disease (see Table 2.1). The combination of forces created a health care system dependent on what the physician defined as illness and the treatment that was needed, including referral for additional treatment or testing, all unbundled from each other and charging for each piece of service without regard for costs, which were escalating impressively in the new regime.

Table 2.1
How Does the Biomedical Model of Health and Illness Differ From a Holistic Model?

Biomedical Model Assumptions	Holistic Model Assumptions
Single underlying cause for a disease; removal of that cause will create health.*	Health and illness are multifactorial; not all abnormalities cause illness, and disease can occur without illness.
Health is the absence of disease.*	Health is a "state of complete physical, mental and social well-being and not merely the absence of disease or infirmity."**
Cure of disease is a goal; death is often viewed as a failure.	To cure and to heal are not the same. It is possible to have a healing death. Death is not an enemy.***
Emotional and mental disturbances are distinct from those of the body.*	There is a unifying interplay between mind and body; they cannot be separated.
The individual is independent of the environment and society.*	The human system is in dynamic, constant interaction with its social, spiritual, and physical environment.
People are victims with little responsibility for illness.*	People are full participants in their health and illness, and their actions and inactions matter. When ill, although not responsible for their condition, they are responsible to it.***
Patients are passive recipients of care.	Patients are active agents in their own recovery and always have choices in how they respond to their health and illness.

Adapted from *Wade and Halligan (2004); **WHO (1946); ***Levine (2010).

ATTEMPTS TO CHANGE FINANCIAL INCENTIVES TO CONTAIN COSTS

Health Maintenance Organizations

There were efforts to change the incentives that accelerate cost, emphasizing wellness and health promotion to contain costs. Notable among these attempts were *health maintenance organizations*, or HMOs. The HMO Act of 1973 was passed during the administration of Republican President Richard Nixon. This model, in its most undiluted sense, is the other side of the coin from fee-for-service. Instead of being reimbursed for each treatment, each service, each Q-tip used, there is a fixed sum per enrollee per month. This is called *capitation* or "by head." All services used must be paid for within this sum. Thus, unlike fee-for-service, which has an incentive for overtreatment and expensive, high-technology care, HMOs have a financial incentive for wellness, with the potential for undertreatment. Thus, early HMOs worked best when the insurance pool covered was largely healthy or had enough "well" members to carry or cover the costs for the sick ones. But physician income could be negatively impacted—remember, unlike fee-for-service setups in which providers treat, bill, and push those costs to third-party payers, HMO models have fixed pools of money to work with. In HMO models in which physicians share the risk for financial loss (more treatment than money gathered per enrolled patient), physicians bore the cost not only of their own decision making but also that of other providers in their group. The impression of fewer services was also decried by many in the public at large who, largely unaware of the overtreatment potential fueled by fee-for-service, felt that this model of financing and reimbursement resulted in a lower quality of care. For these and other reasons, HMOs, which grew in the 1990, faded in prominence thereafter (Bodenheimer & Grumbach, 2012).

Prospective Payment and Diagnostic Related Groups

Concerns about rising costs also caused Medicare to reconsider reimbursement strategies. In 1983, Medicare moved away from fee-for-service reimbursement to prospective payment via diagnosis-related groups, commonly known as DRGs. Instead of hospitals being paid "per diem"—reimbursed for each day that the patient was hospitalized—hospitals were now prospectively reimbursed a lump sum per episode of hospitalization. Ponder the difference in the incentives in these two models. In one, per diem, the hospital is paid for each day the patient is hospitalized. The author, for example, recalls being hospitalized for 3 full days for an uncomplicated wrist fracture in 1966, a procedure that required only simple casting and today would be managed in an hour or two in an outpatient setting. The treatment strategy has not changed, nor is the difference in hospitalization time due to new technology or novel healing strategies. Instead, in the per diem model, hospitals had an incentive for long hospitalizations and did not bear any financial risk for the efficiency with which the care was provided. Indeed, not only was there no incentive for efficient services but there was also a financial incentive for inefficient provision of care. Providers, both the hospital and physician, were generously reimbursed in these years. The advent of Medicare DRGs shifted the financial risk for the length of stay to the hospital.

Nursing Student: 1976—pre-DRG

Mary is excited to start her first clinical rotation at Big City Hospital. She is assigned just one patient, Mrs. Jensen, a 66-year-old having her gall bladder removed. Nurse faculty shares with Mary that faculty selected Mrs. Jensen because she is 2 days pre-op. Mary will have a chance to practice her interview skills with a lucid, well patient—a good start. Mrs. Jensen will have her pre-op lab test tomorrow, as well as a chest x-ray, as is standard for all patients undergoing surgery.

The advent of DRGs dramatically changed this scenario because DRGs are based on a *prospective payment* in a set sum, rather than *retrospective payment* on a per diem rate. Therefore, before DRGs, the hospital would be reimbursed for each day Mrs. Jensen was in the hospital. The physician could solely decide how long she would stay in the hospital. The physician had no incentive for a timely discharge, and the hospital had an incentive to keep the patient as long as reasonably possible.

FINANCIAL INCENTIVES IN DRGs

Just as per diem reimbursement incentivized long hospital stays, the DRG payment scheme incentivizes early discharge. There are labor costs associated with a hospital stay—nurses and others—and the hospital now had the financial incentive to discharge the patient as quickly as possible because reimbursement would be the same, but the cost of care would be much less if the hospital stay were short. Conversely, in a very long stay, the hospital would actually lose money, as the cost of care would be greater than the reimbursement. If instead the patient could be moved through the hospital stay very quickly and the cost of providing care were less than the sum received from Medicare, the hospital would make money on that admission. The speed at which a patient can be moved through a hospital or other setting—admission to discharge—is called *throughput*.

IMPACT OF DRGs

Did this prospective, payment-by-diagnosis strategy impact the growth of health care expenditures, and how did it impact quality? Early reports suggested that this fundamental change slowed the growth of hospital inpatient costs, without an impact on mortality rates and readmission (Davis & Rhodes, 1988). Later analyses found that although there was no impact on a long-standing trajectory toward better hospital care, there was an impact on patient stability at discharge (Kahn et al., 1991). The increase in readmission of patients—presumably due to being discharged too early—was clearly identified over time. Rau (2012) notes:

> With nearly one in five Medicare patients returning to the hospital within a month of discharge, the government considers readmissions a prime symptom of an overly expensive and uncoordinated health system. Hospitals have had little financial incentive to ensure patients get the care they need once they leave, and in fact they benefit financially when patients don't recover and return for more treatment.
>
> Nearly 2 million Medicare beneficiaries are readmitted within 30 days of release each year, costing Medicare $17.5 billion in additional hospital bills. The national average readmission rate has remained steady at around 19 percent for several years, even as many hospitals have worked harder to lower theirs. (p. 1)

Starting in October 2012, hospitals whose 30-day postdischarge readmission rate is above a certain threshold are fined by Medicare. In the first year of the program, 2,217 hospitals forfeited more than $280 million in Medicare funds (Rau, 2012). This ACA policy action addresses what was an unintended consequence of payment by diagnosis, specifically the possibility of premature discharge with a resulting rehospitalization.

Clearly, patients can be harmed by a hospital discharge before they are ready. But recall also that there is harm related to keeping the patients in the hospital too long. This harm is in the form of excessive costs of care that are collectively borne by taxpayers (Medicare and Medicaid admissions) and employers and employees (commercial employer–based private insurance).

Nurses have an opportunity to play a key role in preventing readmission through patient education and discharge planning.

THE ACA AND NEW (AND RENEWED) PAYMENT MODELS

The ACA, passed in 2010, attempts to address many of these issues and is a historic milestone. Along with Medicare and Medicaid in 1965, it is the first major piece of health reform legislation since the many failed attempts starting with Franklin D. Roosevelt (Morone, 2010). Designed to assure that all Americans have financial access to health care, it also incentivizes new patterns of innovation and redesigned care models. Thus, it not only proposes to finance health care in new, more comprehensive ways ensuring coverage for all, but also intends to change reimbursement. This latter aspect, changes in reimbursement strategies, is termed *payment reform.* Payment reform seeks to dramatically change provider behavior. Therefore, to effectively lead in a changing health care environment, nurses must understand the financial incentives and disincentives in a reformed care system. As just one example, nurses can play a leading role in preventing readmission of patients to the hospital and are in a prime position to redesign care models to ensure this end. Therefore, it is valuable to understand just how important this is in the hospital's bottom line when articulating a planned care change.

How Does the ACA Assure Financial Access to Health Care?

The ACA financing model builds on the existing employer-based health care system to assure that all Americans have financial access to health care. In general, universal coverage may be financed in three ways. These are

1. Publicly funded through taxes, often called *single payer*
2. Funded through a requirement that all employers offer health insurance and requiring workers to sign up for this insurance (called an *employer mandate*)
3. Funded through a requirement that all individuals have health insurance (called an *individual mandate*)

The ACA uses all three approaches. Different nations have used various combinations of these and other financing models. Switzerland, for example, uses an individual mandate as its financing vehicle to achieve universal financial access for all its citizens, while Canada uses a single-payer vehicle. It is important to note, however, that each nation's health care system reflects the values and historical evolution within that nation and its culture. Therefore, even when using similar financing mechanism, the health care system may spawn very diverse provider behaviors because of different reimbursement strategies. As one example, Canada's single-payer system reimburses providers in a fee-for-service system, so—while publicly funded through taxes—it retains the potential for the opportunities and challenges inherent in fee-for-service systems.

Currently in the United States, political views about a single-payer system are polarized. Nevertheless, the popular Medicare system is essentially a publicly funded single-payer system for those over age 65. Similarly, Medicaid is a publicly funded (federal with state match) single payer for the poor and disabled.

The ACA takes an approach to financing health care that includes individual mandates and employer mandates. It also retains the Medicare and Medicaid systems, yet allows for testing of new, innovative means to organize, deliver, and reimburse care. Thus, the ACA is not "socialized medicine," in which health care is publicly funded through taxes, and health care workers are employees of the state. Nor is it a publicly funded fee-for-service system like Canada's that unlinks health insurance from employment status (single payer), but reimburses using a fee-for-service methodology. Instead, the ACA includes an employer mandate through the requirement that employers with more than 50 employees provide health insurance coverage for their employees or pay a penalty. For those who are not covered by another means, it includes an individual mandate. To help those individuals who need to purchase insurance to meet the mandate, *health insurance exchanges* enable individuals and businesses to compare and contrast both cost and services so they can make informed decisions. These health insurance exchanges have been set up at the federal level, but a state may opt out and create its own health exchange.

There also was an ACA provision to create a uniform floor for eligibility for Medicaid, but it did not withstand a Supreme Court challenge to its constitutionality. Traditionally, states have had considerable say in determining eligibility standards, such as setting a level of poverty that makes a family Medicaid eligible. The ACA instead required Medicaid eligibility for all individuals/families falling below 133% of the federal policy–level poverty, and states could still choose to have expanded eligibility beyond that. In a legal challenge to the ACA, however, the Supreme Court issued a June 28, 2012, decision that, in essence, made states' expansion of Medicaid optional.

The passage of the ACA heralded new payment models that aim to decrease costs while improving quality. New and renewed nursing skills are needed to optimize these payment models. These are discussed in Chapter 3.

Thought Questions

1. What might the U.S. health care system look like if the Flexner Report was never written?

2. Why do some Americans support Medicare, yet oppose governmental involvement in health care?

3. What are the strategies that enable universal financial access to health care? Is one strategy better than others? Why or why not?

4. Define the following key terms:

   Capitation

   Health maintenance organizations

   Payment reform

   Per diem reimbursement

   Retrospective reimbursement

   Throughput

   Unbundled services

Exercises

1. Prepare a short presentation on the evolution of the health care system in the United States, from the early 1900s to the present day.

2. Develop a presentation on the pros and cons of the three financing approaches in the Affordable Care Act.

Quiz

TRUE OR FALSE

1. One characteristic of the biomedical model is that the concept of *health* includes physical, mental/emotional, spiritual, and social aspects.

2. In the early 1900s, hospitals were the most highly preferred settings for medical treatment.

3. In response to the Flexner Report, nursing became a more highly compensated profession, with resulting increased social status for nurses.

4. The first U.S. employer-based health insurance was offered to Dallas schoolteachers for six dollars a year.

5. The American Hospital Association established Blue Cross, which enabled insurees to have a choice of hospitals.

6. Blue Shield was established to ensure physician reimbursement for care provided.

7. National health insurance was considered for inclusion in the original Social Security Act during the administration of President Franklin D. Roosevelt.

8. Medicare and Medicaid were enacted in 1965 as a potential solution to the unintended consequences of employer-based health insurance.

9. Hospital nursing services have largely remained bundled into hospital room charges.

10. Capitated reimbursement within *health maintenance organizations* creates the same treatment incentives as fee-for-service reimbursement.

MULTIPLE CHOICE

11. Holistic models of health
    A. Consider *health* to be the absence of disease
    B. Consider the human mind–body interplay and the interplay of the mind–body with physical, social, and spiritual environments
    C. Both A and B
    D. Neither A nor B

12. Which of the following is *not* true: As a result of the Flexner Report,
    A. Medical education became longer and more expensive
    B. Medical education opportunities for women and people of color increased

    C. Most of the programs in homeopathy, naturopathy, and osteopathy were forced to close

    D. Physician specialization rather than primary care was emphasized

13. Employer-based insurance
    A. Grew dramatically due to wage and price controls during World War II
    B. Is a pretax fringe benefit
    C. Excludes retired and unemployed individuals
    D. All of the above

14. The enactment of Medicare and Medicaid within fee-for-service reimbursement
    A. Fueled rapid growth in the health care industry
    B. Fueled unbundling of services, so that each piece of health care service would be charged individually
    C. Both A and B
    D. Neither A nor B

15. Medicare
    A. Began paying hospitals prospectively by diagnosis-related groups starting in 1983
    B. Is publicly funded through payroll taxes
    C. Both A and B
    D. Neither A nor B

16. Hospital reimbursement via diagnosis-related groups
    A. Financially incentivizes long hospital stays
    B. Creates the potential for premature hospital discharge of patients
    C. Removes incentives to enhance hospital throughput
    D. All of the above

17. The Affordable Care Act financing model includes
    A. Public funding through taxes
    B. Employer insurance mandates
    C. Individual insurance mandates
    D. All of the above

18. The health insurance exchange
    A. Is intended to help individuals and small businesses compare different insurance plans
    B. Began with the Health Maintenance Organization Act during the administration of President Nixon
    C. Both A and B
    D. Neither A nor B

NOTE

1. This is a true story based on the author's father.

REFERENCES

Barkin, S., Fuentes-Afflick, E., Brosco, J., & Tuchman, A. (2010). Unintended consequences of the Flexner report: Women in pediatrics. *Pediatrics, 126*, 1055–1057.

Bodenheimer, T., & Grumbach, K. (2012). *Understanding health policy: A clinical approach*. New York, NY: Lange/McGraw Hill.

Davis, C., & Rhodes, D. (1988). The impact of DRGs on the cost and quality of health care in the United States. *Health Policy, 9*(2), 117–131.

DeLew, N. (2000). Medicare: 35 years of service. *Health Care Financing Review, 22*(1), 75–102.

Duffy, T. (2011). The Flexner report—100 years later. *Yale Journal of Biology and Medicine, 84*, 269–276.

Harley, E. (2006). The forgotten history of defunct black medical schools in the 19th and 20th centuries and the impact of the Flexner report. *Journal of the National Medical Association, 98*, 1425–1429.

Kahn, K., Draper, D., Keeler, E., Rogers, W., Rubenstein, L., Kosecoff, M., . . . Brook, R. (1991). *The effects of the DRG-based prospective payment system of quality of care for hospitalized Medicare patients. Executive summary*. Santa Monica, CA: RAND Corporation.

Levine, S. (2010). *Healing into life and death*. New York, NY: Knopf Doubleday Publishing Group.

Morone, J. (2010). Presidents and health reform: From Franklin D. Roosevelt to Barack Obama. *Health Affairs, 29*(6), 1096–1100.

Order of Saint Benedict. (n.d.). *The rule of Saint Benedict*. Retrieved July 30, 2014, from http://www.osb.org/rb/

Prislin, M., Saultz, J., & Geyman, J. (2010). The generalist disciplines in American medicine one hundred years following the Flexner report: A case study of unintended consequences and some proposals for post-Flexnerian reform. *Academic Medicine, 85*, 228–235.

Rau, J. (2012). Medicare to penalize 2,217 hospitals for excess readmissions. *Kaiser Health News*. Retrieved August 5, 2014, from http://www.kaiserhealthnews .org/Stories/2012/August/13/medicare-hospitals-readmissions-penalties .aspx

Stahnisch, F., & Verhoef, M. (2012). The Flexner Report of 1910 and its impact on complementary and alternative medicine and psychiatry in North America in the 20th century. *Evidence-Based Complementary and Alternative Medicine, 2012*, Article ID 647896, doi:10.1155/2012/647896

Starr, P. (1982). *The social transformation of American medicine: The rise of a sovereign profession and the making of a vast industry.* New York, NY: Basic Books.

Sultz, H., & Young, K. (2011). Hospitals: Origin, organization, and performance. In *Health care USA: Understanding its organization and delivery* (7th ed.). Sudbury, MA: Bartlett and Bartlett Learning.

Wade, D., & Halligan, P. (2004). Do biomedical models of illness make for good healthcare systems? *British Medical Journal, 329*(7479), 1398–1401.

World Health Organization (WHO). (1946, June). *Preamble to the Constitution of the World Health Organization.* Paper presented at the International Health Conference, New York, NY. (Signed on 22 July 1946 by the representatives of 61 States [*Official Records of the World Health Organization*, no. 2, p. 100]).

PAYMENT REFORM

CHAPTER 3 DETAILS payment reform models and describes the impact on the roles, responsibilities, and knowledge needs of RNs. Following completion of this chapter, you will be able to

- Describe the limitation of fee-for-service reimbursement for health care services
- Illustrate essential dimensions of emerging payment models along a range from more, such as fee-for-service, to the other end of the continuum, global capitation
- Discuss essential nursing knowledge in the reformed health system

Cissy has enjoyed her 12 years as an RN in the surgical intensive care unit (ICU) of a community hospital. She is aware that changes seem to be happening, and there are rumblings of financial strain at the hospital. Cissy is glad that all of that has nothing to do with her. Her indifference was shattered when the Chief Nursing Officer invited Cissy and two other ICU nurses together for a meeting. Chief Nurse opens by sharing that Cissy and her colleague have been exemplary nurses, but that they will "soon be dinosaurs." "The inpatient book of business is shrinking," Chief Nurse states, "and we need to downsize that portion of our workforce or lay people off." Cissy is stunned—and defensive! Chief Nurse details the hospital situation with terms Cissy has not become familiar with: "shared savings programs," "bundled payments," and "per member per month global budgets." Chief Nurse concludes with the following statement: "I don't want to lose you three…how about retooling for transitional care?" Flash-forward one year later: Cissy loves her new role managing transitions for the chronically ill population in the hospital service area.[1]

The previous chapters detailed the rise of the medical establishment within the fee-for-service milieu. Incentives in fee-for-service systems push toward higher volumes and thus reward or incentivize *more* care rather than *better* care. Fee-for-service models incentivize behavior that fragments care and create disincentives for coordination and integration. Fee-for-service also contributes to the nation's difficulty containing health care costs. Thus, payment reform, a key element of health care reform, is creating new and different incentives and disincentives than we have seen previously in health care. Understanding emerging payment models helps nurses make sense of the clinical arena, and their own work, as it did for Cissy. Understanding incentives and disincentives is also necessary to provide leadership in the redesign of health care. To aid understanding, the models for payment reform described in this chapter are presented along a continuum from most like fee-for-service to progressively less like fee-for-service and ending with global budgets. Note, however, that these models are in flux, and the exact elements may vary from setting to setting or state to state.

FROM VOLUME TO VALUE: PAYMENT MODELS THAT MOVE AWAY FROM FEE-FOR-SERVICE REIMBURSEMENT

Six models are detailed. These are *pay for performance* (*P4P*); *advanced primary care*, which is also known by the term *patient-centered medical home; accountable care organizations* (*ACOs*) and accountable care *shared savings programs* (*SSPs*); *bundled payments*, sometimes called *payment by episode* or *episode payment models*; and hospital *global budgets*.

Pay for Performance

P4P builds on fee-for-service by providing additional financial incentives to providers who achieve quality metrics (see Box 3.1). It is an attempt to better align the business case with the case for quality within the clinical setting. It is not an alternative to fee-for-service, but instead provides complementary,

---

Box 3.1

What Are Quality Metrics?

Concepts such as *health* or *good care* can be difficult to define and measure. Quality metrics use something that can be measured to serve as a proxy for health, health improvement, efficiency, or effectiveness. Some metrics focus on outcomes, while others focus on process. Still others may measure the patient experience, including patient satisfaction. By using metrics, individuals, organizations, health systems, or nations may compare their performance relative to peers as well as those they aspire to be like. In some settings, individual providers such as nurse practitioners and physicians in patient-centered medical homes can compare their performance and cost with their peer providers. On the other end of the spectrum, the United States can compare the performance of U.S. health care with that delivered in other nations. Comparison can be a powerful incentive toward improvement; no one—whether an individual, organization, or nation—wants to be the highest cost entity delivering lower quality care. This form of comparison is termed *benchmarking*.

---

additional reimbursement when selected metrics are met. This additional reimbursement can occur at the individual (typically physician) level, a group-of-providers (again usually physicians) level, or the institutional level. The logic for additional reimbursement for achievement of certain quality and outcome metrics is that under fee-for-service, poor-quality care receives the same compensation as high-quality care. In some cases, poor-quality care receives more reimbursement than high-quality care, and errors, inefficiencies, and unnecessary care are all reimbursed, indicating a mismatch between the providers' financial incentives and patient needs. P4P injects the new variable of objective measures of quality that theoretically promote better alignment between provider behavior and better outcomes for patients. At the same time, P4P does not require that providers take on financial or other risks for their clinical judgments and behaviors. Instead, it relies on measures that are intended to be an objective reflection of their performance. As such, this small step in payment reform is more palatable to some providers. Moreover, although a small step, it is a radical move away from the relative lack of accountability inherent in the fee-for-service system.

A challenge in P4P—indeed, in any payment system linked to outcomes—is the choice of metrics. There is the potential for metric-driven behavior (Mannion & Braithwaite, 2012) that results in metric-driven patient harm (Rambur, Vallett, Cohen, & Tarule, 2013). Examples of behavior that can lead to metric-driven harm include gaming and measure fixation (see Box 3.2 for a full list). In addition, to date, the outcomes of P4P are mixed, with some studies finding quality improvement (Calikoglu, Murray, & Feeney, 2012) and others finding no improvement in quality when compared to hospitals not under a P4P system (Ryan, Blustein, & Casalino, 2012). Similarly, studies in other settings such as nursing homes did not find consistent improvement using P4P models (Werner, Konetzka, & Polsky, 2013). Finally, as Van Herck

---

Box 3.2
Metric-Driven Unintended Consequences

Tunnel vision refers to the prioritization of financially incentivized care over other valuable care or a prioritization of measured elements of care over unmeasured care of equal or greater value.

Measure fixation is a focus on particular measurement without reflection on how maximization of the particular outcome can miss or even be in opposition to the underlying objective of care. It also refers to focus on a particular measurement without attention to the distress caused to a patient by maximization of the metric.

Acontextual actions or cherry picking refers to the potential to choose patients who can maximize positive measurement while deferring or refusing to treat more vulnerable, more seriously ill patients.

Misrepresentation refers to the deliberate *manipulation of data* so that the reported behavior differs from the actual behavior.

Gaming refers to *manipulation of behavior* to meet targets. It differs from misrepresentation in that it is a contortion of *actual* behavior, not merely *reported* data.

Myopia refers to a focus on short-term, measurable performance at the expense of legitimate long-term consequences and goals.

Suboptimization is the pursuit of narrow local objectives by managers at the expense of the objectives of the organization as a whole.

Ossification is the inhibition of innovation. It may include organizational paralysis brought about by an excessively rigid system of performance measures.

Adapted from Smith (1995).

and colleagues (2010) noted in a systematic review of the P4P literature, programs resulted in "the full spectrum of possible effects … from absent or negligible to strongly beneficial" (p. 1476). Clearly, the verdict on P4P is not yet in.

Finally, it could be argued that physicians and other providers should inherently strive for quality, as many do, rather than needing additional financial incentives to do so. From this perspective, a system like P4P may be an inherently ethically flawed approach. To illustrate the ethical knot, ponder the following: An analogy to P4P would be paying for college with tuition funds, but if it could be demonstrated that a student actually learned not only what was expected but also beyond that, then the faculty member or the faculty group teaching in that discipline would receive additional compensation. A system in which providers need to be incentivized to embrace quality outcomes seems antithetical to fundamental ethical principles like *beneficence* and professional responsibility. We return to this issue of ethics and, specifically, *ethinomics*, the intersection of ethics and economics, in Chapter 7.

Patient-Centered Medical Homes

Unlike episodic, physician-centric care, the idea behind patient-centered medical homes is that comprehensive personalized care can best be delivered by a team (see Figure 3.1). This team may include different combinations of skills sets for different patients and includes the use of registries and electronic health record data for individual and population-based care. The use of these data can in turn help the medical home determine which patients are in need of some aspect of care. Patient-centered medical homes also rely on *community health teams* and *health coaches* for an array of supportive services. Community health teams were defined in the Affordable Care Act to potentially include "medical specialists, nurses, pharmacists, nutritionists, dieticians, social workers, behavioral and mental health providers (including substance use disorder prevention and treatment providers), doctors of chiropractic, licensed complementary and alternative medicine practitioners, and physician assistants" (American College of Physicians, 2013, p. 1), whereas health coaches are individuals who work with patients to change behavior and improve health. The overall premise is that such an approach will create higher quality care at a lower cost.

Despite logical elegance, studies do not fully support the founding hypothesis of higher quality, lower cost care as a result of this model. A 3-year pilot study with 32 primary care practices, 6 health plans, and roughly 120,000 patients did not find a reduction in patients' use of hospitals or emergency departments (EDs) or a reduction in total cost of care in this model, and found only limited improvement in quality. At the same time, the

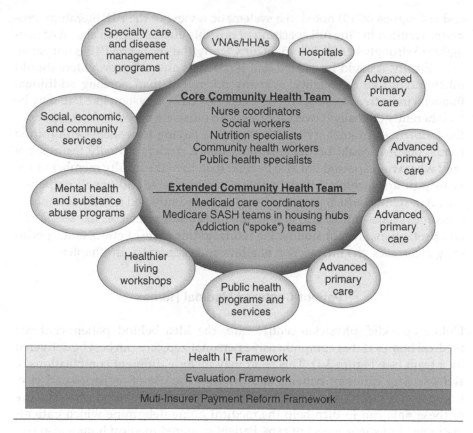

Figure 3.1
Patient-centered medical home.
Adapted from Department of Vermont Health Access (2014).

primary care physicians in the participating practices received accumulated average bonuses of $92,000 per physician during the 3-year trial (Friedberg, Schneider, Rosenthal, Volpp, & Werner, 2014). Nielson, Olayiwold, Grundy, and Grumbach (2014), however, report improvement in many metrics including cost across 20 studies.

It is quite possible that the fundamental approach is sound, but the settings with poor results are either not constituted optimally or that there has not been sufficient time to achieve high-quality, lower cost care. As illustrated in Figure 3.1, *teamness* is a central construct in a patient-centered medical home, yet the optimal nature and composition of the teams awaits explication. A documented challenge in implementing truly comprehensive team-based care includes the physician-centric nature of many practices and unimaginative roles for nurse practitioners and physician assistants (Nutting, Crabtree, & McDaniel, 2012). Thus, some of the less-than-expected outcomes may relate to team composition or function, particularly given that other settings demonstrate success to date (Department of Vermont Health Access, 2014), such as lowered cost without a negative impact on quality. This model includes the following components:

1. A foundation of medical home and community health teams that support coordinated care between and among a broad array of services and provider types
2. A health information infrastructure that includes electronic medical records, hospital data, a health information exchange network, and a centralized registry so all can access information about the patients in their care
3. Payment reform that includes commercial insurance, Medicare, and Medicaid to support the medical home/community team approach
4. Routinely collected data as part of an evaluation infrastructure to guide service delivery, improve quality, and assess program impact

As depicted in Figure 3.1, this approach is not focused on acute and episodic care (although such care is provided), but instead includes a broad array of programs and services. These include, for example, *support and services at home* to encourage aging in place, commonly known as *SASH*, community-based self-management program, and *hub and spoke programs* for opioid treatment, to name but a few elements. Note, however, that the specific supports and services are not prescriptive and reflect the needs of the population served. A service area with a high proportion of elderly would need a different overall composition and provision of services than one with a high proportion of families of childbearing age. Thus, such an approach is not rooted solely in a medical model of treatment, but spans social support and other services inclusive of population, family, and individual needs. As such, the configuration of the community health team also varies to align with the health and well-being needs of the target population. Moreover, populations with particular needs will receive care tailored to those needs. To illustrate just one targeted need, the hub and spoke model for treatment of opioid addiction spans a range of supports (see Figures 3.2 and 3.3). This single yet very nuanced service illustrates the complexity and integration needed to provide patient-centered services in a system that initially evolved in response to a fee-for-service environment.

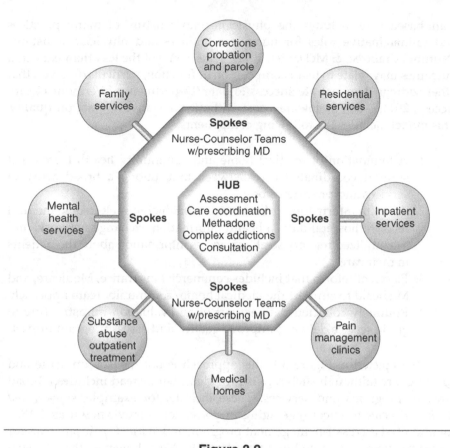

Figure 3.2
Integrated health system for addictions treatment.
Adapted from Department of Vermont Health Access (2014).

How well have patient-centered medical homes worked? Systematic meta-analysis has been challenging due to the variability of definitions and approaches, with early evidence supporting positive patient and staff experiences of care (Jackson et al., 2013). Similar to P4P, further research that informs the cost and effectiveness of this approach lies in the future.

Accountable Care Organizations

The Affordable Care Act provided the impetus for the formation of ACOs. ACOs are an attempt to shift the locus of care to a population, with a focus on *value of service* rather than *volume of service*. In this way, ACOs—at least

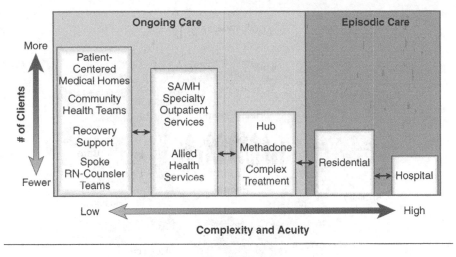

Figure 3.3
Continuum of health services for addictions treatment.
Adapted from Department of Vermont Health Access (2014).

theoretically—are a dramatic departure from fee-for-service, which incentivizes volume of care over the actual value of that care. This challenges nurses to a new manner of thinking; just because services are being provided (volume) does not mean that this treatment has value.

An ACO may be further defined as a group of providers who have agreed to be accountable for the cost and quality of care for a defined population. Although these terms do not seem revolutionary in and of themselves, this is indeed a radical departure from the traditional fee-for-service approach in which accountability for cost was largely absent, and aggregated accountability for outcomes was loose, at best, and frequently nonexistent. Moreover, ACOs typically depend on complex data management, aiding the analysis of both cost and quality (see Figure 3.4), and the sophistication required to create and maintain the necessary supporting software and hardware is a relatively new capacity in the health care arena and is still underdeveloped in many places, making ACOs difficult without that support.

Importantly, ACOs are not health maintenance organizations (HMOs). In fact, elements of ACOs emerge from what had been viewed as failures or limitations in HMOs. An ACO, for example, does not limit beneficiaries' access or choice of providers, and there is no *gatekeeper*. The term gatekeeper refers to an element of HMOs in which patients cannot directly access specialists or any provider other than their primary care provider, who need to refer the patient if the services are to be covered financially by the third-party payer.

Figure 3.4
Accountable care organization structure.
Adapted from Xcenda, an AmerisourceBergen company. Used with permission.

ACCOUNTABLE CARE SSPs

ACO SSPs take the ACO model a bit further by allowing savings from innovation and care redesign to be shared between the providers and the payer. Such funding provides a financial bridge between treatment cultures rooted in volume of treatment as the marker of financial success—the "more is better" model—and new ones referencing a more complex mix of quality and cost outcomes. Specifically, SSPs differ from a traditional fee-for-service arrangement in a number of important ways. First, it is a *performance-based contract* between a *payer* (such as private insurance or Medicare) and a *provider organization* that will share savings from delivery of more cost-effective care between the payer and provider. The assumption is that the potential for financial return will drive innovation, coordination, and redesign of care processes and infrastructure. Care coordination and redesign is an area where there is substantial opportunity for nurses to influence the value of care.

Nancy is an RN in a clinic that is part of a physician–hospital organization that employs 1,500 physicians. The clinic is affiliated with an academic medical center, and most of the physicians have admitting privileges. Nancy is concerned about inefficiencies in the patient scheduling process. She completes a literature review and identifies two models that could be more efficient. She shares these with her supervisor, who then asks Nancy to present her findings and recommendations to the senior leadership team. They adopt Nancy's redesigned model for flow and patient throughput. The subsequent performance data suggests that Nancy's model results in far shorter waiting periods for patients with emergent conditions and higher patient satisfaction, with an overall reduction in unexpected hospital admissions for acute exacerbations in patients with chronic conditions. Because overall expenditures were less than projected, the clinic group receives a portion of these savings. Nancy knows it took someone "on the ground" and close to the working surface to see both the problem and the potential for such an innovative solution. As a result of her excellent work, Nancy is promoted to a new role, Direction of Innovation. A key responsibility is to interact with staff nurses to identify and implement workflow redesign as well as clinical service delivery innovations that decrease unnecessary utilization of services, reduce overall costs, and meet key quality metrics.

Sharing Savings

So, how is the amount that could be shared determined? The payer and ACO, guided by quality targets that must be met, determine the projected expenditures—expenditures expected in a traditional fee-for-service delivery model—for a population of patients. These projections are *risk adjusted*, meaning the expenditure projections take into consideration the health and illness status of the population. Thus, the model recognizes that a group that is more ill typically uses more services and incurs higher costs. Then, over time, the actual expenditures are compared with the projected expenditures, and any savings are then shared by predefined formulas (see Figure 3.5). Note that quality targets must be met. The cost savings cannot be at the expense of quality.

What if the new models actually fail to yield savings or the actual expenditures are higher than expected? This latter is termed *downside risk*. The acceptance of downside risk would mean that the provider groups would be held financially accountable for some portion of expenditures above the projection (see Figure 3.6). In the traditional fee-for-service models of health

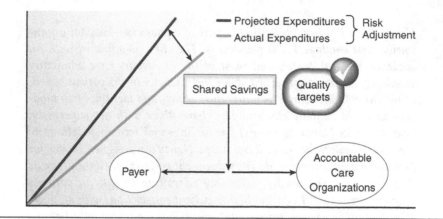

Figure 3.5
Calculating shared savings.
Courtesy of Kara Suter, M.S. Used with permission.

care, that extra cost is instead reflected in higher insurance premiums the next year. Acceptance of downside risk places provider groups in the situation of being financially accountable not only for what goes right, receiving some portion of the saving, but also financially accountable for some of the excessive cost if things do not go well. Although Medicare pilot trials designed to test shared savings ACOs allow providers who accept downside

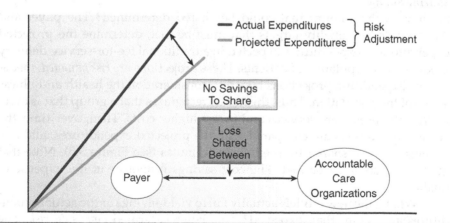

Figure 3.6
Shared savings illustrating downside risk.

risk to keep more of the profits, by late 2013, roughly 90% of the Medicare ACOs did not accept the downside risk option. It is important to understand that this downside risk does not simply evaporate. In the Medicare situation, for example, excessive costs are borne by taxpayers. In the private insurance market, these costs will be borne by the insurance company in the short term, but passed on to those insured in the form of higher premiums. Thus, the contribution nurses can make toward positive redesign, and the value of such redesign, is substantial. Specific skills are detailed in a later portion of this chapter.

Bundled Payments

In contrast to P4P, patient-centered medical homes, and ACOs that are variants of fee-for-service, bundled payments replace fee-for-service payment and its incentives with a fixed amount by episode, condition, or insured life. Bundled payments typically target types of care that have been expensive or populations that are frequent users of health service, for example, those diagnosed and frequently admitted with congestive heart failure (CHF). In a fee-for-service system, there is no incentive to, for example, keep a patient out of the ED, use palliative care when appropriate, or provide nurse and social worker support to the individual and the family. Indeed, the types of services not provided by someone who can bill, for example, an RN rather than an MD, are uncompensated in fee-for-service.

In bundled payment models, integrated care delivery is incentivized. Care for a CHF patient may include the hospital, home health nurses, skilled nursing faculty, and specialty physicians as necessary. The care provided by the hospital, however, would look very different than in a fee-for-service system. The hospital may hire nurses to specifically develop individualized plans of care with ongoing support to keep these patients out of the hospital. *Superutilizers* have been a successful target of such nursing-based coordinated care.

Superutilizers represent just 1% of the U.S. population, yet they are responsible for 22% of the cost. In Medicaid, this imbalance is even more dramatic; 5% of the population represents 55% of the cost (Mann, 2013). One successful model employs teams of nurses and social workers for individual *and* population management. Such care depends on the use of robust data, and strong analytic skills are needed by the field-based care managers and care coordinators. Using this approach, the Vermont Chronic Care Collaborative, for example, has demonstrated promising early results, with $11.5 million in savings after expenses, an 8% reduction in inpatient utilization, a 4% decrease in ED utilization, and 11% decrease in 30-day read-mission rate (Mann, 2013). Mann also notes common characteristics across successful programs, such as:

1. **Web-based provider portals with easy access to patient data.** These data can then be used to discern patterns of health care utilization, such as when there is a visit to the ED versus a primary care visit. Understanding individual patterns of utilization provides the foundation for development of tailored interventions for each patient.
2. **Real-time data.** This is useful to develop effective, tailored, strategies for care management. Any lags in data must be minimal. ED utilization reports from 6 months to a year ago would not help a care coordinator develop timely interventions to address the root cause of the ED visits.
3. **Decision-support tools.** These can help the care manager use the data in meaningful ways, supporting the transition from information to knowledge to a plan for action by offering prompts to action under defined conditions of data patterns.

Other studies have found that bundled payments for the management of cancer resulted in a 34% decrease in the expected cost, but a paradoxical increase in the cost for chemotherapeutic agents. Nonetheless, it still netted dramatic overall cost savings with no alteration in quality (Newcomer, Gould, Page, Donelan, & Perkins, 2014). This study was also testing the sharing of physician performance information as a means to enhance quality, raising the potential that physician behavior changed because outcomes were being measured. As a result, the differential impact of bundled payments alone cannot be discerned, with the final verdict on bundled payments yet to be determined. Nevertheless, this payment strategy offers refreshing promise. Nurses, with broad education across different populations and settings, coupled with their understanding of human behavior and analytics, are in a powerful position to maximize the potential of bundled payments.

Global Budgets

Global budgets take many of the incentive forces in bundled payments to the next level by bundling all services in a particular setting, such as hospitals. Global budgets mean all-payer (Medicare, Medicaid, and commercial insurance) payments to hospitals and their employed physicians, based on the *historical revenue* for a defined period of time, usually a year. You can think of the concept of historical revenue as analogues to your income from the previous year. Although the hospitals will be guaranteed their revenue for the upcoming year, they will have significant incentives to reduce avoidable utilization, coordinate care better, and manage their costs in order to enhance the quality of care and improve their margins or the amount that remains after they have paid their expenses. Over time, of course, the hospital budget may need to increase to reflect legitimate increases in expenses (e.g., raises for the nurses) within an overall orientation of cost control. Thus, as a means to control the growth in health care spending, increases in a hospital's global budget from year to year should be based on economic indicators that reflect the overall growth in the economy, such as the consumer price index, market basket index, or gross state product. Another approach to global budgets would be to reimburse hospitals on a risk-adjusted *per member per month* (*PMPM*) method.

Overall, the incentives in global budgets are very different from the volume-based incentives under fee-for-service reimbursement. Quality performance measures and efficiency standards can be incorporated into the global budget formula to modify overall payments over time, offering additional incentives for enhancement of the quality of care.

Why would a setting such as a hospital consider a global budget? Slusky, Weppler, and Murray (personal communication, December 19, 2013) offer the following perspectives.

Unlike fee-for-service payments, global budgets provide the participating hospitals predictable revenues, while at the same time incentivizing the hospital to focus more on cost management rather than revenue enhancement. Global budgets are also a way to link the payment system to the goals of population-based health care. Over time, a global budget can reflect the total amount a community ought to be spend, based on the demographics and health care needs of the population being served by the hospital and other community providers. A hospital reimbursed in a global budget model in a region with many families of childbearing age, for example, would likely offer dramatically different combinations of services than a hospital serving a large community of elders. Providers also have greater flexibility to determine how to spend human and capital resources to meet community needs. And, like a household budget, the hospital has strong incentives to reduce unnecessary care and care of little value, particularly if it is expensive, invasive care.

Maryland has experimented with all-payer rate setting through a Medicare waiver for decades. However, in 2014, the state of Maryland negotiated a new Medicare waiver that requires the state to implement hospital global budgets within a 5-year period. The intent of this approach in Maryland is to control the growth of health care expenditures over time based on a predetermined trend factor and provide incentives for the hospitals to increase their margins by better management of their costs, relative to their budgets.

NURSING ROLES WITHIN EMERGING PAYMENT MODELS

Emerging payment models offer tremendous opportunities for nurses to bring their knowledge, skills, and abilities into play in new ways. Educated across provider settings—hospitals, nursing homes, and home health practice specialties, and at individual, family, and population levels—the generalist scope of practice of a baccalaureate or higher degree RN is an excellent fit with the societal need to address health care cost. Indeed, nurses have the potential to be the glue in the new health system. Some skills are new domains for nurses, whereas others are not new, but rather renewed skills, preparation, and education that are dormant. Notably, in the fee-for-service system, a nurse is viewed as a *labor cost* rather than a *knowledge worker*. The emerging models recognize that all care is a cost, and unlike in fee-for-service, in which physicians and hospitals are perceived as *revenue drivers* creating cash flow, these models recognize the parallel societal cost better.

Are nurses ready to lead care redesign within new payment models? Fraher, Ricketts, Lefebvre, and Newton (2013) argue that too little attention has been given to the learning needs of those who are not physicians. These authors suggest:

> [B]ecause of sheer numbers—the U.S. health care system employs 2.7 million registered nurses—it is nurses who are arguably in the most pivotal position to drive system change . . . . Nurses are providing patient education and care coordination, improving care transitions between community and acute care settings, conducting home visits for patients with complex chronic conditions, enhancing patient and family engagement, improving population health management, and increasing community outreach. These efforts have reduced unnecessary hospitalizations and readmissions, improved patients' experiences, increased the quality of care provided, and lowered costs. (p. 1813)

In the post–fee-for-service world, these outcomes matter, demanding fresh attention to the skills needed in today's health care system. Skills such as "prevention, care coordination, care process reengineering, dissemination of best practices, team-based care, continuous quality improvement, and the use of data to support a transformed system" (CMMI, cited in Fraher et al., 2013, p. 1813) are well suited to nurses' skill sets and interests, yet demand a broad and deep understanding of health economics. Thus, Section II (Chapters 4 through 6) expands on the foundation developed in Chapters

1 through 3 to further explicate the nuances of health economics as foundational nursing knowledge in the emerging era. To aid understanding and application, health economics is illustrated in contrast to examples of classic economics that are common in nurses' everyday lives.

Thought Questions

1. In which payment mode would you prefer to be?
   a. A 28-year-old with poorly controlled type 1 diabetes
   b. An elder with multiple chronic conditions
   c. A pediatric neurosurgeon
   d. An RN

   Provide a rationale for each response.

2. What are the potential unintended consequences of each of the payment reform models?

3. Define the following key terms:

   Accountable care organization

   Benchmarking

   Global budget

   Patient-centered medical home

   Pay for performance

   Risk adjusted

   Shared savings program

Exercise

1. Develop a presentation to explain payment reform models to your peers, including a description of how each model works, its value to society, and its strengths and weaknesses.

Quiz

TRUE OR FALSE

1. All forms of reimbursement create the same treatment incentives and disincentives.

2. The acronym P4P refers to a form of health care financing termed *preferred for payment.*

3. Another term for patient-centered medical homes is advanced primary care.

4. The Affordable Care Act defined potential members of the community health team.

5. The optimal configuration of team members in a patient-centered medical home has been defined and is firmly supported by empirical evidence.

6. An accountable care organization may be defined as a group of providers who agree to be accountable for the cost and quality of the care provided.

7. The term *superutilizer* refers to individuals who use a disproportionally high amount of health care.

8. Hospital global budgets provide hospitals with a predictable revenue outlook.

9. Under fee-for-service reimbursement, nurses are often viewed by management as a labor cost.

10. Bundled payments create a financial incentive to coordinate care across the entire episode of illness or condition management.

MULTIPLE CHOICE

11. Fee-for-service reimbursement
    A. Creates strong incentives for care coordination
    B. Contributes to the nation's difficulty containing health care costs

C. Both A and B
D. Neither A nor B

12. Linking reimbursement to achievement of quality metrics
    A. May result in better health care outcomes
    B. May create metric-driven behavior that creates metric-driven patient harm
    C. Both A and B
    D. Neither A nor B

13. In addition to employing physicians and nurses, patient-centered medical homes rely on
    A. Community health teams
    B. Health coaches
    C. Both A and B
    D. Neither A nor B

14. One of the ways accountable care organizations differ from health maintenance organizations is
    A. There are no gatekeepers in accountable care organizations
    B. Accountable care organizations do not limit beneficiaries' access to health care or choice of providers
    C. Both A and B
    D. Neither A nor B

15. Accountable care organization shared savings programs
    A. Create opportunities for nurses to influence the value of care provided through care coordination and care redesign
    B. Require that quality thresholds be met before savings from expected expenditures are shared among the payer and the accountable care organization
    C. Both A and B
    D. Neither A nor B

16. Global budgets in health care
    A. Create financial incentives to reduce avoidable health care utilization
    B. Create financial incentives to coordinate care
    C. Both A and B
    D. Neither A nor B

17. Fee-for-service reimbursement
   A. Creates financial incentives to reduce avoidable health care utilization
   B. Creates financial incentive to coordinate care
   C. Both A and B
   D. Neither A nor B

18. Nursing skills valued in a reformed health care system include
   A. Care process reengineering
   B. Care coordination
   C. The use of data
   D. All of the above

NOTE

1. True story, shared with the author in May 2014.

REFERENCES

American College of Physicians. (2013). *Community health teams to support the patient centered medical home.* Retrieved August 18, 2014, from http://www.acponline .org/advocacy/where_we_stand/assets/ii12-community-health-teams.pdf

Calikoglu, S., Murray, R., & Feeney, D. (2012). Hospital pay-for-performance programs in Maryland produced strong results, including reduced hospital-acquired conditions. *Health Affairs, 31*(12), 2649–2658. doi:10.1377/hlthaff.2012.0357

Department of Vermont Health Access. (2014). *Vermont blueprint for health: 2013 annual report.* Retrieved February 20, 2015 from http://hcr.vermont.gov/sites/ hcr/files/pdfs/VTBlueprintforHealthAnnualReport2013.pdf

Fraher, E., Ricketts, T., Lefebvre, A., & Newton, W. (2013). The role of academic health centers and their partners in reconfiguring and retooling the existing workforce to practice in a transformed health system. *Academic Medicine, 88*(12), 1812–1816. doi:10.1097/ACM.0000000000000024

Friedberg, M., Schneider, E., Rosenthal, M., Volpp, K., & Werner, R. (2014). Association between participation in a multipayer medical home intervention and changes in quality, utilization, and costs of care. *Journal of the American Medical Association, 311*(8), 815–825. doi:10.1001/jama.2014.353

Jackson, G., Powers, B., Chatterjee, R., Bettger, J., Kemper, A., Hasselblad, V., . . . Williams, J. (2013). The patient-centered medical home: A systematic review. *Annals of Internal Medicine, 158*(3), 169–178.

Mann, C. (2013, July 24). *Targeting Medicaid super-utliizers to decrease cost and improve quality*. Baltimore, MD: Centers for Medicare and Medicaid Services (CMCS Informational Bulletin).

Mannion, R., & Braithwaite, J. (2012). Unintended consequences of performance measurement in healthcare. *Internal Medicine Journal, 42*(5), 569–574.

Newcomer, L., Gould, B., Page, R., Donelan, S., & Perkins, M. (2014). Changing physician incentives for affordable, quality cancer care: Results of an episode payment model. *Journal of Oncology Practice, 10*(5), 322–326. doi:10.1200/JOP.2014.001488

Nielson, M., Gibson, J., Buelt, L., Grundy, P., & Grumbach, K. (2015). *The patient-centered medical home's impact on cost and quality: An annual update of the evidence 2013–2014*. New York, NY: Milbank Memorial Fund.

Nutting, P., Crabtree, B., & McDaniel, R. (2012). Small primary care practices face four hurdles—including a physician-centric mind-set—in becoming medical homes. *Health Affairs, 31*(11), 2417–2422. doi:10.1377/hlthaff.2011.0974

Rambur, B., Vallett, C., Cohen, J., & Tarule, J. (2013). Metric-driven harm: An exploration of unintended consequences of performance measurement. *Applied Nursing Research, 26*(4), 269–275.

Ryan, A., Blustein, J., & Casalino, L. (2012). Improvement among low-performing hospitals: Medicare's flagship test of pay-for-performance did not spur more rapid quality. *Health Affairs, 31*(4), 2417–2422.

Smith, P. (1995). On the unintended consequences of publishing performance metrics. *International Journal of Public Administration, 18*(2–3), 277–310.

Van Herck, P., DeSmedt, D., Annemans, L., Remmen, R., Rosenthal, M., & Sermeus, W. (2010). Systematic review: Effects, design choices, and context of pay-for-performance in health care. *BMC Health Services Research, 10*(1), 247. doi:10.1186/1472-6963-10-247

Werner, R., Konetzka, R. T., & Polsky, D. (2013). The effect of pay-for-performance in nursing homes: Evidence from state Medicaid programs. *Health Services Research, 48*(4), 1393–1414. doi:10.1111/1475-6773.12035

HEALTH CARE ECONOMICS: AN OVERVIEW

Health care markets differ from classic free markets in dramatic ways. Why is knowing this important to you? Many elements of health care and health reform are shaped by policy or payment attempts to either add elements of classic free markets to health care markets or correct or control consequences of the manner in which health care markets work. Simply put, it is difficult to understand much of what happens in health care without understanding these principles. Fortunately, these principles and their consequences are easy to understand when they are contrasted with principles of classic free market theory that you are familiar with in your everyday life.

Chapter 4 describes a principle you are very familiar with: When you purchase something, you notice the price because you are paying for it, and the purchase is felt in your pocketbook. Health care differs in important ways, and these are detailed.

Chapter 5 describes the central role of information in classic markets, how health care markets differ from these, and the emerging trends that are increasing the role of information in health care policy and nursing practice.

Chapter 6 reviews two more principles that manifest along a range of things familiar to you—such as the licensing law that enables you to practice as an RN—to less familiar but important things like Certificate of Need and antitrust laws.

Together, this information will enable you to understand better the things happening in your workplace and clinical setting as well as clarifying overall principles of health reform. Importantly, it also provides an essential framework by which to understand health care and policy changes long into the future.

4

HOW HEALTH CARE MARKETS DIFFER FROM CLASSIC MARKETS

CHAPTER 4 BUILDS on the foundation in Chapters 1 through 3 to more fully explicate the nuances of health economics. To do so, health care markets are described in contrast to classic free markets. Following completion of this chapter, you will be able to

- Contrast the implications of "the buyers bear the consequences of their decisions" between classic free markets and health care markets and decision making
- Explain key related strategies such as cost sharing
- Discuss the concept of demand in health care, including supply-induced demand

WHAT DOES IT MEAN TO BEAR THE CONSEQUENCES OF FINANCIAL DECISION MAKING?

The opening two scenarios illustrate the first item.

June Jones, RN, is exhausted after a 12-hour shift and decides a bit of "retail therapy" is in order. She stops at the local upscale department store on her way home from work. There she is captivated by a pricey watch she sorely desires. Recalling that the rent is due as well as the payment on her son's orthodontics, she decides to forgo the new watch. Determinedly, she also marches past the clothing sale rack, carried by the realization that right now she cannot afford anything new. What she has will simply have to do.

Ms. Williams enters the emergency department with vague symptoms following a fall while skiing. Although she was wearing a helmet, Ms. Williams recalls a famous actress who died after a ski injury. Ms. Williams is worried. The emergency department triage finds nothing unusual, but Ms. Williams is very vocal in her concern, her anxiety accelerating. The busy attending physician, Joan Garcia, MD, plans watchful waiting with clear instructions on warning signs, but at Ms. Williams's insistence, reconsiders. As Ms. Williams blathers, Physician Garcia's attention shifts to the recent department meeting in which the fiscal status of the hospital was reviewed: Patient revenues are down, her department chair shared, and targets for higher inpatient volumes have been set. Thumbing the chart, Dr. Garcia notes that Ms. Williams has low-deductible, fee-for-service insurance. The waiting room is filled with patients needing immediate attention, and Dr. Garcia is eager to move on to the next patient. As she tries to move on, Ms. Williams attaches herself, barnacle-like, adamant that she wants a complete checkup. She slyly suggests that she "just may sue if not treated right." Although Dr. Garcia is convinced it probably is not necessary, she orders a CT scan. Ms. Williams now seems very happy with her care, calling to tell her son she likely will be admitted.

These scenarios illustrate one of the significant ways in which health care markets differ from classic free markets. In a classic free market, *buyers bear the financial consequences of their decisions to purchase* a product or service. The value of each potential purchase is weighed against other appealing options as well as other financial responsibilities. As a result, buyers *self-ration* purchases all the time. Few Americans, for example, drive a Rolls-Royce. It is simply too expensive a car for most people, and perhaps not even practical. Instead, cars are purchased with an appreciation of the impact of the cost of purchase in relationship to other purchase opportunities, as well as the value of the potential purchases in relationship to other goods and services. Nurse Jones, for example, weighed the impact of the cost and value of a new watch and wardrobe against other responsibilities and desires. She chose not to make a purchase. Nurse Jones self-rationed. Similarly, an individual considering a new car will weigh the pros and cons of different options—different makes and models, new or used, current vehicle or public transportation—based on the cost and perceived value of the contribution the new purchase brings.

Less-Immediate Cost Consequences in Health Care

Conversely, Ms. Williams had little incentive to moderate her desire for care. Ms. Williams does not bear the immediate financial impact of her decision to seek services. It is a bit like asking someone looking for a car if they want a Rolls-Royce and handing them the keys, or like a parent or other authority deciding that a Rolls is for you and handing you the keys. In each case, the cost of this interaction is largely hidden from view.

Ms. Williams may perceive that the services are "paid for anyway" by the insurance company. This arrangement masks the cost of seeking services, and thus there is little self-rationing among those with health insurance, in part because the immediate cost of the decision to purchase is not borne by the consumer. Indeed, the cost may even be difficult to ascertain. Similarly, the actual value of the service is very difficult to determine, and one of the things the patient is "purchasing" is information itself. As Arrow (1963) notes, "When there is uncertainty, information or knowledge becomes a commodity" (p. 946). The role of information in markets is a critical issue that is discussed in depth in Chapter 5.

Third-Party Payers

Simply put, Ms. Williams did not weigh the cost of treatment against her other financial demands. She showed up at the emergency department expecting treatment. Unlike a classic free market where the interaction is limited to two entities, a buyer and seller, health care includes a *third party*. This third party is insurance companies; indeed, insurance companies are called *third-party payers* for exactly this reason.

Third-party payers exist to spread risk, in the ways described in Chapter 1. At the same time, the cost of treatment is not apparent or visible to the individual because he or she does not bear that cost immediately and directly, nor can he or she read it on a price tag. Instead, that cost is spread to the group. Indeed, spreading the cost of care from the individual to many is the functional purpose of insurance groups to begin with. Insurance companies spread the risk, a strategy that can keep down individual financial risk and—if the individual is in a low-utilization group—cost of insurance. Yet, if there is a great deal of high-cost utilization within the group, insurance rates will increase the following year. Nevertheless, this event is chronologically disconnected from the individual's decision to seek treatment at a certain time, and the cost is an aggregate based on the sum of all care provided within a group that year.

The Value of Providers Assuming Financial Risk

The providers in a fee-for-service system also have no incentive for nontreatment or for limiting the cost of treatment. Recall that the *cost* borne by the insurance company—which is actually borne by the members in the group through their premiums--is actually *revenue* to the provider. Thus, there is a misalignment between incentives, highlighting the importance of risk sharing in payment reform (see Box 4.1).

Health Care as a Vulnerable Purchase

There are other key ways health care markets differ from classic free markets, and many of these make it difficult to control costs. Unlike other goods and services, health care is a vulnerable purchase. In a classic market, purchasing power is in the hands of the consumer. A consumer may buy what and when he or she wants and walk away from a purchase without consequences. Nurse Jane, for example, although desirous of the flashy watch, does not bear dramatic consequences for not making the purchase, desire and disappointment notwithstanding. For Ms. Williams, however, things are more muddled.

Box 4.1
What Is Payment Reform?

Payment reform is the umbrella term used to define health care reimbursement strategies that move away from fee-for-service, as described in Chapter 3. These include, for example, pay-for-performance, accountable care shared savings programs, bundled payments, and global budgets. Inherent in these strategies is *provider accountability* for selected outcomes and—in the case of the latter three—cost of clinical decision making. This is in contrast to fee-for-service, in which providers are not held financially accountable for the cost, or value, of their treatment decisions.

Although it is quite possible that Ms. Williams is best left untreated, it is also possible that she has anything from a concussion to a basilar skull fracture. Health care "purchases" are marked by *uncertainty*. This notion was first promulgated by Kenneth Arrow, the Nobel Prize–winning economist whose seminal ideas birthed the area of health care economics referenced in Chapter 1.

UNCERTAINTY AS AN ECONOMIC CONCEPT

Thus, unlike Nurse Jane who could easily ascertain the rewards and costs of the new watch, Ms. Williams cannot be certain about what she needs. She cannot assess what is unnecessary, what the potentially harmful consequences of actions and options are, and what the potentially harmful consequences of inaction are. Indeed, some of what Ms. Williams is seeking in health care is exactly this information. Dr. Garcia, although processing more information, also cannot be fully certain of the consequences of either course. Arguably, the instinct of most Americans—both providers and patients—is toward treatment even if the final result is overtreatment-induced harm. Without financial risk sharing, providers also have few incentives and face organizational disincentives for watchful waiting, provided the patient—like Ms. Williams—has insurance that will cover the cost of care. Treatment momentum accelerates when patient satisfaction is an outcome metric and the patient clearly desires treatment. Unlike a classic free market in which assumption of the financial risk of the purchase moderates consumption, neither the provider nor the patient have an incentive to limit, or even question, treatment.

The scenario illustrated in the preceding text details an employer-based insurance scenario. Nevertheless, similar treatment incentives hold in all fee-for-service systems, including tax-funded ones like Medicare. Cassidy (2013), for example, notes that the current fee-for-service reimbursement scheme in Medicare "gives beneficiaries little incentive to see the highest value care or avoid unneeded care" (p. 4).

Strategies Connect Patients to Financial Consequences of Treatment

Strategies to encourage consumers of health care to be cognizant of the cost of their actions exist and are well known to nurses. These include deductibles, copayments, and coinsurance (see Box 4.2). Together these are termed *cost sharing*. Notably, the Affordable Care Act (ACA) has attempted to incentivize certain care by eliminating or subsidizing cost sharing for certain interventions or individuals. A child visiting a provider for immunizations, for example, would not have a copayment, while a sick child visit may, depending on

---

Box 4.2

Types of Cost Sharing

Deductible: The amount an individual needs to pay out of pocket before the insurance company begins its coverage for services.

Copayment: A payment owed by the individual at the time a covered service is received.

Coinsurance: A form of ongoing cost sharing between an individual and an insurance company in which the individual pays a percentage of covered services.

---

the specifics of the plan. The overall policy objective is to remove disincentives for needed care, but not unneeded care.

Deductibles, the amount an individual needs to pay out of pocket before the insurance company begins its coverage for services, are arrayed along a continuum from low to high, each with different utilization disincentives. There are plans with comparatively low deductibles—for example, Medicare Part B at $147/year or employer-based insurance at $250/year/family. For individuals and families in which this is the only form of cost sharing, there is no disincentive to health care use once this relatively low bar for cost has been reached. High deductibles of up to $5000 to $10,000 per family per year offer a substantial disincentive, even for needed care. The ACA has addressed this and mandates *maximum out-of-pocket* or *MOOP* limits. These are set annually by the federal government; for example, the 2015 MOOP for a single person is $6,600 and $13,200 for a family plan (Healthcare.gov, n.d.). Some states have additional out-of-pocket limits by category, for example, for prescription drugs. In the ACA, limits are aggregated into the overall MOOP. How does cost sharing impact the use of health services? How does it impact health? Well, it depends.

Cost Sharing: A Barrier to Needed Care or Opportunity to Decrease Unnecessary Utilization?

Sarah Jones has a stomachache. The persistent nagging pain in her side is now nearly constant, and aggravated with movement. She feels "off"— tired, slightly nauseated, and light-headed. She ponders calling her primary care provider, Ai Le, NP (nurse practitioner), but suspects that the receptionist will just encourage her to see NP Le in the clinic. Sarah likes her provider, but the effort of going to the clinic seems exhausting. She also recalls that her employer-based insurance has just been switched to a high-deductible plan with a copayment due at the time of the visit. Sarah decides to "gut it out" and see how she feels in the morning.

Many individuals make the same decision as Sarah. Indeed, a seminal RAND study found that when comparing those with no cost sharing to those in high-deductible plans, those in the former used 40% more health services (Newhouse, 1993). Does this impact their health? As health providers, it surely seems that what we do should matter and does matter! Surely those individuals who do not seek treatment suffer health consequences? Although it would seem logical, the data does not consistently support negative health outcomes as the result of lower usage. Moreover, recent evidence also suggests that there is substantial overdiagnosis, overtreatment, and even screening-induced harm (Welch, Schwartz, & Woloshin, 2011) in the U.S. system. Sarah's decision to forgo treatment may evolve without further incidents or negative effect.

SELF-LIMITING HEALTH EVENTS

Sarah goes to bed early and is awakened with severe stomach cramps and diarrhea. She recalls the party she was at the night before and wonders if this bout is the result of bad Brie. "Why do I eat things that taste bad?" she laments. She leaves the bathroom feeling better, quickly falls asleep, and awakens refreshed in the morning.

In this scenario, in which Sarah had an acute, self-managed episode, the avoidance of medical intervention is positive.

WHAT ABOUT THOSE WITH CHRONIC ILLNESS?

High-deductible plans have had a different trajectory for those with chronic diseases. Specifically, high-deductible plans have been associated with a significant cost burden for those who, unlike Sarah's acute episode likely of food-borne origin, have chronic conditions and must seek and remain in regular treatment and make visits to their provider (Galbraith et al., 2011).

How Do Deductibles Differ From Copayments?

Copayments, payments due at each visit, have also been associated with decreased use. Numerous studies have found, for example, that even relatively small copayments due at the time of an emergency room (ER) visit have reduced nonemergency utilization of the ER, although this was not found in a study of Medicaid enrollees (Mortensen, 2010). Other studies have found that when comparing no-copayment groups with both low- and high-copayment groups, the two copayment groups were less likely to seek care for minor symptoms, but the high-copayment groups were also less likely to seek care for serious symptoms. Given these findings, it is logical to assume that this copayment consequence would negatively impact health outcomes. Yet in this study, the health status, both physical and mental, was similar among all the copayment groups (Wong, Anderson, Sherbourne, Hays, & Shapiro, 2001), suggesting that there were no long-term adverse effects of copayment cost sharing. But an alternative scenario haunts every clinician.

> *Sarah goes to bed early and is awakened by sharp pains in her shoulder. Almost too weak to stumble to the bathroom, she realizes she is now very, very sick. She calls her friend, who takes her to the ER. Sarah is diagnosed with a ruptured ectopic pregnancy, in which the bleeding is irritating the diaphragm. Nurse Jones tells Dr. Garcia, "This one looks shocky" and Dr. Garcia ponders if Sarah should be admitted to the regular unit or intensive care unit (ICU). "How does someone let something like this go?" wonders Nurse Jones.*

So, which scenario was Sarah headed for? Was the deductible and copayment a reasonable and important and appropriate disincentive for seeking care, or did it prevent Sarah from receiving needed care? To date, the ability to systematically tease out when avoidance of care is positive and when it leads to adverse health outcomes remains elusive. Genuine need for health services, a seemingly straightforward phenomenon, is—like many things in health economics—a complicated issue with entwined components. Fortunately, there are new research strategies and tools, some of which are discussed in the following sections.

WHAT IDEAS HELP US UNDERSTAND OVERTREATMENT?
THE EXAMPLE OF SMALL-AREA VARIATION AND
SUPPLIER-INDUCED DEMAND

An area of study and research called *small-area variation* works toward understanding the relationships among the various components, motivations, and outcomes.

Supply, Costs, and Small-Area Variation

Sandra is frustrated. A social worker with years of experience in a community health center, she is upset that there is so much that could be done for patients that simply is not happening. "Why can't people just get what they need?" she laments.

Sandra seems to be asking a simple question, and on the surface, the answer seems straightforward. Nevertheless, there is a great deal of uncertainty when attempting to dissect what constitutes "need," as well as an evolution in understanding the complexity of this construct.

Even the use of early models of health services differentiated between *perceived need* and *evaluated need* (Anderson, 1968), with evaluated need presumed to correlate with actual need. But this straightforward distinction conceals a complex reality. Eddy (1996) notes that need was once simply defined—it was whatever the physician said it was. Yet, does the fact that it is named by clinician evaluation make it real, actual, or right? Over time and many research studies, it has become increasingly clear that the answer is a resounding "No!" Different providers may offer different diagnoses for the same situation, or—even with the same diagnosis—order different amounts of tests or treatment.

Groundbreaking work (Wennberg & Gittelsohn, 1973) over time led by Jack Wennberg at Dartmouth created a whole new area of investigation around this concept, called *small-area variation*. Small-area variation refers to differing patterns of health care utilization in one region as compared to another, even when controlling for differences in the patients. Small-area variation illustrates that services delivered in response to what is considered need in one part of the country would not be delivered in another. This is not driven by mistakes or incompetence. Instead, it flows from a phenomenon termed *supplier-induced demand*.

WHAT IS SUPPLIER-INDUCED DEMAND?

Wennberg, a physician with a masters in public health studying for a doctorate in sociology, was working in rural Vermont, an ideal laboratory for health services research because of its relatively homogeneity. Pioneering concepts in medical practice epidemiology, Wennberg noted that 70% of children from one Vermont community had tonsillectomies by age 15, while in a community 10 miles away, the proportion of children with tonsillectomies was 20%. On closer examination, there was no logical explanation for this variance. The children were not different in any way that could explain the large discrepancy in the apparent "need" for tonsillectomies.

Utilizing increasingly complex analytic tools over time, one difference between high-utilization areas and low-utilization areas was evident: the numbers and types of providers. Areas with more internists, for example, had patients receiving more diagnostic tests, even when the patient profiles were similar. Areas with more cardiovascular surgeons, in general, had more patients receiving cardiovascular surgery. Thus, the concepts of small-area variation and supplier-induced demand became areas of ongoing scientific inquiry and policy application. Although better accepted today, the notion of overtreatment and anything less than objective clinical decision making was very radical thinking when first introduced.

Unlike Health Care, in Traditional Markets Oversupply Decreases Demand

The importance of this concept is illustrated in contrast to a classic free market in the following scenario.

Jannie is excited! She is going to her first farmer's market selling her mother's homemade fudge. As she wheels into the parking area, she is thrilled by the number of vendors. "This should bring in a ton of customers," Jannie notes with glee. As she sets up her booth, however, her heart sinks. To her left, there is another booth selling fudge. She wheels around to the right. More fudge vendors. Marching to the aisle between rows of booths, she stands with arms akimbo. The farmer's market is booth after booth of fudge vendors, 35 in all. Jannie is totally deflated. With the farmer's market awash in fudge, why would anyone seek out her booth? Jannie knows that with so many people selling fudge, her sales will be almost nil...there is just too much competition!

In a classic free market, when supply is high, costs typically decrease due to market competition. If there is a glut of a product, similar to fudge at Jannie's farmer's market, many items of the product simply will not sell at all. Supplier-induced demand in health care is exactly the opposite: The greater the supply, the greater the use—the more surgeons, for example, the more surgeries. Santerre and Neun (2009) describe the capacity for providers to induce demand for their services as follows:

> [C]onsumers are relatively ill-informed concerning the proper amount of medical care to consume because an asymmetry of information exists regarding the various health care options available. This asymmetry forces consumers to rely heavily on the advice of their physicians for guidance. This implies that physicians are not only providers of physician services but also play a major part in determining the level of demand for those services. For example, physicians advise patients about how frequently they should have office visits, medical tests, and appropriate treatments. This situation places physicians in a potentially exploitative position. Physicians may be able to manipulate the demand curves of patients to advance their own economic interests. (p. 370)

But, as already noted, there is also a growing body of data that does not consistently find better health outcomes with higher utilization. Taken as a whole, this suggests that the typical relationship among supply, quality, and cost containment that is considered basic in traditional economics simply cannot be transferred to health care, which has, among other effects, fueled the experimentation with new payment models as detailed in Chapter 3.

Hypotheses about regional differences in utilization as a result of supplier-induced demand have led to policy questions about differential payment by geographic regions, to reward appropriate utilization and lower cost. However, as Wennberg, Barne, and Zubkoff (1982) noted early on, these differences are likely due to differences in the way providers diagnose and treat. This hypothesis was further supported in a complex, broad Institute of Medicine (IOM, 2013) study that included not only Medicare, but also commercial insurance usage. This IOM report further confirmed the presence of substantial geographic variation in treatment rates and costs, without a consistent relationship between these variables and quality of care or outcomes for the patients. They recommend that these be addressed by targeting clinical decision making, clinical and financial integration, and coordination of services. Finally, information about the product, health care, is essential to economic decision making. However, as Arrow noted in 1963:

The value of information is frequently not known in any meaningful sense to the buyer; if, indeed, he knows enough to measure the value of information, he would know the information itself. But information, in the form of skilled care, is precisely what is being bought from most physicians, and, indeed, from most professionals. The elusive character of information as a commodity suggests that it departs considerably from the usual marketability assumptions about commodities. (p. 946)

This seminal statement remains sound, yet is even more complex and nuanced, given the explosion of information-sharing technology and processes and contemporary policy initiatives such as "meaningful use." Thus, we will turn our focus to information, economics, and health care in Chapter 5.

Thought Questions

1. Imagine you are a healthy 30-year-old male. For you, what are the pros and cons of a lower monthly insurance premium with higher cost sharing, versus a higher monthly premium with lower cost sharing?

2. Imagine you are a 62-year-old female with multiple chronic conditions. For you, what are the pros and cons of a lower monthly insurance premium with higher cost sharing, versus a higher monthly premium with lower cost sharing?

3. To what extent should patients feel a financial impact when they seek care? How can needed care best be separated from unnecessary care? Provide a rationale for your answer.

4. To what extent should providers be accountable for the cost and outcomes of care that they recommend? Provide a rationale for your answer.

5. Define the following key terms:

   Maximum out-of-pocket limits

   Self-rationing

Small-area variation

Supplier-induced demand

Third-party payer

Exercise

Develop a presentation for your peers that details the ways in which the decision to use health care is similar to other decisions and the ways it is different. Explain the relationship of these to the contemporary reform era.

Quiz

TRUE OR FALSE

1. In a classic free market, consumers bear the financial consequences of their decision to purchase a product or use a service.

2. Insurance companies are also called third-party payers.

3. In fee-for-service reimbursement models, providers have little incentive to limit treatment or consider the cost of treatment.

4. In health insurance, a deductible is another term for a copayment.

5. One way health care markets differ from classic free markets is that in a classic free market, oversupply decreases demand and enhances cost and quality competition.

6. The term *asymmetry of information* means that consumers have less information about health care options than physicians, and physicians can therefore influence demand for health services.

7. Need for health care services is a clearly defined phenomenon.

8. Individuals with high-deductible health insurance plans uniformly have worse health outcomes than those with low-deductible health insurance plans.

9. The Affordable Care Act attempts to incentivize some care by removing the cost share for the service.

10. Cost sharing and cost shifting refer to the same phenomenon.

MULTIPLE CHOICE

11. Cost sharing
    A. Refers to copayment and deductibles
    B. Is a strategy to encourage consumers of health care to consider the cost and value of care when using/purchasing health care services
    C. Both A and B
    D. Neither A nor B

12. Small-area variation
    A. Refers to differing patterns of health care utilization in one region as compared to another, differences that occur even when controlling for differences in the patients
    B. Refers to different types of hospitals in rural versus urban settings
    C. Both A and B
    D. Neither A nor B

13. Maximum out-of-pocket limits
    A. Cap the amount of health care costs an individual or family pays in a single year
    B. Were put into place with the passage of the Affordable Care Act
    C. Both A and B
    D. Neither A nor B

14. Third-party payers
    A. Spread financial risk among individuals in the insurance pools
    B. Are called third parties because they are not the first or second party, that is, not the buyer or seller
    C. Both A and B
    D. Neither A nor B

15. The cost of health care
    A. Is borne by society in the financial form of taxes or insurance premiums
    B. Is actually revenue to the provider
    C. Both A and B
    D. Neither A nor B

16. The concept of supplier-induced demand
    A. Was heralded by the work of Jack Wennberg
    B. Suggests that the supply of health care providers rather than genuine need for health care services drives at least some use of health services
    C. Both A and B
    D. Neither A nor B

REFERENCES

Anderson, R. (1968). *A behavioral model of families' use of health services* (Research Series No. 25). Chicago, IL: University of Chicago Press.

Arrow, K. (1963). Uncertainty and the welfare economics of medical care. *American Economic Review, 53*(5), 941–973.

Cassidy, A. (2013, June 20). Health policy brief: Restructuring Medicare. *Health Affairs.* Retrieved from http://www.healthaffairs.org/healthpolicybriefs/brief.php?brief_id=95

Eddy, D. (1996). *Clinical decision making: From theory to practice.* Boston, MA: Jones & Bartlett.

Galbraith, A., Ross-Degnan, D., Soumerai, S., Rosenthal, M., Gay, C., & Lieu, T. (2011). Nearly half of families in high-deductible health plans whose members have chronic conditions face substantial financial burden. *Health Affairs, 30*(2), 322–331.

HealthCare.gov. (n.d.). Out-of-pocket maximum/limit. Retrieved February 20, 2015, from https://www.healthcare.gov/glossary/out-of-pocket-maximum-limit

Institute of Medicine (IOM). (2013). *Variation in health care spending: Target decision making, not geography.* Washington, DC: National Academies Press.

Mortensen, K. (2010). Copayments did not reduce Medicaid enrollees' nonemergency use of emergency departments. *Health Affairs, 29*(9), 1643–1650.

Newhouse, J. (1993). *Free for all? Lessons for the RAND health insurance experiment RAND Corporation.* Cambridge, MA: Harvard University Press.

Santerre, R., & Neun, S. (2009). *Health economics: Theories, insights, and industry studies.* Mason, OH: South-Western Cengage Learning.

Welch, H. G., Schwartz, L. M., & Woloshin, S. (2011). *Overdiagnosed: Making people sick in the pursuit of health.* Boston, MA: Beacon Press.

Wennberg, J., Barne, B., & Zubkoff, M. (1982). Professional uncertainty and the problem of supplier-induced demand. *Social Science and Medicine, 16,* 811–824.

Wennberg, J., & Gittelsohn, A. (1973). Small area variations in health care delivery. *Science, 182*(4117), 1102–1108.

Wong, M., Anderson, R., Sherbourne, C., Hays, R., & Shapiro, M. (2001). Effects of cost sharing on care seeking and health status: Results from the medical outcomes study. *American Journal of Public Health, 91*(11), 1889–1894.

5

THE ROLE OF INFORMATION IN HEALTH CARE MARKETS AND DECISION MAKING

THIS CHAPTER DETAILS how information is used by consumers to make decisions that, in aggregate, may enhance quality while reducing cost, in contrast to health care markets in which this information is more difficult to access and understand. The evolution of emerging strategies to support information access is detailed. Following completion of this chapter, you will be able to

- Describe the role of information in economic decision making
- Discuss emerging health care trends such as evaluation science, health information exchanges, price transparency, and "big data"
- Consider new and emerging roles for RNs in a data-rich world

THE NEED FOR INFORMATION

Philip, a nurse, has a problem. He worked hard to save enough money for a down payment on his condo, picking up extra shifts at the hospital and using public transportation rather than getting a car. It has been worth it! Philip loves his new home. Now settled in for three months, Philip was just finding financial breathing room, or so he thought. Now this!

Three times in the past three weeks Philip has found water streaming out of his dishwasher and onto the floor. Now there is a stain in the basement ceiling, so Philip knows the leak is serious, and his attempts at home repair did not work. Philip considers his options: (a) Wash all dishes by hand in soapy water; (b) call a repair person; or (c) buy a new dishwasher.

Philip needs more information to make a decision. He calls the repair shop, and the manager tells Philip that a visit by a repair technician will cost a minimum of $125. Moreover, there may be parts that are needed and a second visit, so the total cost is unclear. Philip then visits a local appliance shop as well as several discount stores and a warehouse. He compares the cost of the different models as well as the features. He then looks online for more product information and is surprised to find that one of the "off-brand" models is actually made by the same company as a highly rated brand name; in fact, it is the same dishwasher, just with a different label. Finally, Philip checks the different store policies on delivery and installation and finds that several of the stores offer these as a free service. Philip now feels confident he accurately knows the cost of the different options. Philip has all the information he needs to make the best decision possible, or at least the decision that is best for him.

Similarly,

Sandi stops by the local grocer after her clinical rotation at a primary care office. She notices that the store brand of canned green beans is almost 30 cents cheaper than the name brand. "How bad can they be?" she asks herself as she picks up the store brand. In the next aisle, Sandi pauses in front of the coffee. There is a much cheaper brand than what she is using, but Sandi's boyfriend, Howard, likes Fancybrand and Sandi decides to stick with it. Saturday morning coffee is just too precious to mess with, Sandi decides as she puts Fancybrand coffee in her cart.

Classic free markets rest on a foundation of information. As Philip's experience exemplifies, the consumer knows about the product or knows how to obtain information. Information sources may include consumer guides, or stars and "thumbs up" on websites, or may be rooted in past experience. Indeed, shoppers sort through information informed by their own experience on a daily basis, as Sandi's example illustrates. When purchasing green beans, for example, the shopper can sort out the pros and cons of the less-expensive store brand and the one with the fancy label. Moreover, except for very large purchases, the impact of a choice with an undesirable outcome can be easily rectified. If Sandi buys the cheaper store brand and does not like it, she can go so far as to toss it out and make a different decision next time without much financial or quality-of-life impact. Notably, the buying power is in the hand of the individual consumer, not the seller, because— after thinking about the pros and cons as well as the impact of the expense on the capacity to obtain other goods and services, as discussed in the previous chapter—the buyer can walk away.

Buying Power and Vulnerability

Health care is dramatically different. First, unlike the power a consumer has in a classic free market, as noted in the previous chapter, health care is a *vulnerable purchase.* A mother whose child has lost consciousness and cannot be roused after a hard fall in the playground, for example, does not have the option of taking time to review the treatment pros and cons, costs, and likely outcomes on the way to the emergency department. Moreover, the cost of inaction may prove life threatening, unlike if Philip decides to forgo a dish- washer, which would result in a small investment from him of kitchen time with hands in soapy water each day.

Asymmetry of Information and Supplier-Induced Demand

Second, unlike a classic market in which the consumer has information about the product or knows how to obtain it, the consumer of health care usually goes to the provider to obtain information, for example, a diagnosis or prog- nosis. This *asymmetry of information* (Arrow, 1963) does not exist in classic free markets in which the power is in the hand of the consumer. Moreover, once a patient is seen, the provider can also control the *demand* for health care, by ordering tests, offering referral or specialty services, surgery, and repeat visits, and the patient is not in a position to easily discern what is necessary and what is not. Instead, the patient trusts that what the provider states is right, necessary, and in the patient's best interest. As detailed in Chapter 4, there is substantial evidence (Mulley, 2009; Dartmouth Atlas, n.d.) that this *supplier-induced demand* creates large variations in care in different parts of the country, even when the differences between patients are controlled. The mag- nitude of a health care provider's capacity to induce demand for services is largely unique among all U.S. goods and services. As Wennberg, cited as "the creator of modern evaluative science" (Mullan & Wennberg, 2004, VAR 73) states, "Lurking behind variations in patterns of care are often huge hospital investments in expensive technologies that are directly tied to their economic stability" (VAR 79). In other words, expensive investments in facilities and technologies must be paid for, and a "build it and they will come" orientation has prevailed. This sort of information is not readily accessible to a patient who is trying to determine what health services he or she needs. At a broader level, resources like *The Dartmouth Atlas of Health Care* documents "glaring variations in how medical recourses are distributed and used in the United States" and can be used to shape health policy and examined by health analysts.

Price Transparency

Another unique element of the health system relates to a different piece of information a wise consumer needs: cost. Imagine a grocery store in which there are no prices listed on anything in the store, and when store workers are asked what things cost, they respond, "I don't know." Imagine if when told you needed an injection, your first question was, "How much will it cost?" What *do* individual health care services cost? What does the care you provide, as a nurse, cost the patient? The taxpayers?

This seemingly simple question is surprisingly complicated in health care and is at the heart of an issue called *price transparency*. Recall from Chapter 4 that buyers self-ration their own purchases in classic free markets because the buyer knows that she or he will bear the impact of the decision making. Information is central to making that decision. Philip may decide to "self-ration" and not replace his dishwasher. Conversely, he may decide to go with one of the purchase options. In all cases, he has the opportunity to know the cost impact and weigh his decision accordingly. Similarly, imagine driving along a busy roadway hunting for a gas station. How would you decide which one to go to if prices were not posted? What would impel gas station owners to practice any type of cost containment if both you and they thought you could pass those costs off to someone else? Yet there is a much greater difference in the cost of the same health services in a) different settings and b) by payer type than there is in gas prices.

Price Variability

In health care, the situation is even more complicated because a second answer to the "How much does it cost?" question is, "It depends." Different employer groups negotiate to obtain discounted fees. Large employers, therefore, have an advantage in negotiating lower rates. In addition to different prices secondary to negotiated rates, different facilities charge dramatically different amounts for the same goods or services. In reflection, Dentzer (2013) notes:

> What does U.S. health care have in common with an exotic international bazaar? The prices at either one are almost never posted, whether for a heart bypass operation or an antique rug. And the final price will also most certainly have little to do with the seller's opening bid.

Despite hospital charges having been set prospectively via diagnosis-related groups (DRGs) since 1984 (see Box 5.1), nearly ninefold differences in average hospital charges were evident in a Centers for Medicare and Medicaid Services analysis (Dentzer, 2013). In a similar vein, Ginsburg (2010) found that some providers, particularly hospitals for their inpatient services,

---

Box 5.1

Reminder: What Is the Prospective Payment,
Diagnosis-Related Groups (DRGs)?

Prior to the adoption of prospective payment for hospitalized Medicare patients in 1984, hospitals were reimbursed retrospectively for whatever they would decide to charge, including a per diem—meaning by the day—charge for each day of hospitalization. Reform was necessary to prevent insolvency, and the new model paid hospitals a fixed rate based on the diagnosis or combination of diagnoses (Mayes, 2007). In this manner, although the federal government via Medicare retained financial risk for the overall number of hospital admissions, the hospital assumed financial risk for the length of stay (Bodenheimer & Grumbach, 2012). Mayes notes that "the change was nothing short of revolutionary. For the first time, the federal government gained the upper hand in its financial relationship with the hospital industry. Medicare's new prospective payment system with DRGs trigged a shift in the balance of political and economic power between the providers of medical care (hospitals and physicians) and those who paid for it— power that providers had successfully accumulated for more than half a century" (p. 21).

Box 5.2

What Is Shared Decision Making?

The Informed Medical Decisions Foundation defines shared decision making (SDM) as "a collaborative process that allows patients and their providers to make health care decisions together, taking into account the best scientific evidence available, as well as the patient's values and preferences" (Informed Medical Decisions Foundation, undated website). Lee and Emanuel (2013) submit that it is a "sleeper provision of the Affordable Care Act" (p. 6) and particularly useful for circumstances in which there is not a clear, single best treatment option, thus enabling optimal, informed alignment with the patient's values and wishes.

---

were able to negotiate "higher-than-market" prices, meaning "higher than everyone else." Ponder the contrast with markets that are more familiar, such as a restaurant that charges much more for roughly the same meal, service, and ambience. This sort of difference would be easily discernible to the savvy diner, but is very difficult for the consumer of health care to recognize.

The Role of Patient Choice

Further, when one considers how individuals create links in their thinking among price transparency, cost, value, and *patient choice*, additional complexity is introduced. Sommers, Dorr Gould, McGlunn, Pearson, and Danis (2013), for example, found that patients tend to equate higher cost with higher quality, even when the higher cost care is not higher in quality. Moreover, these researchers identified substantial barriers to shared decision making (SDM; see Box 5.2) with reference to cost (see Box 5.3). They conclude that substantial efforts to broaden patient understanding will have to be complemented by greater provider preparation in being informed about and in being able to discuss the cost of care with a patient. Do you feel comfortable talking to patients about cost? How would you go about gaining those skills?

DATA ON QUALITY

Clearly, transparency in pricing is just one element of the sort of information consumers need to make wise decisions. Another key element is clear information about quality. Despite challenges that include difficulty identifying

---

Box 5.3

Barriers to Shared Decision Making That Is Inclusive of Cost

1. Patients want what they perceive as the best care and assume that the most expensive care is the best possible care.
2. Patients perceive that the most expensive is the best even when there are other available alternatives with acceptable outcomes that are less expensive. A patient, for example, may perceive an expensive highly advertised brand name pharmaceutical to be more effective than a bioidentical generic medication.
3. Patients have little experience in considering health cost trade-offs—what they are getting and what they are giving up by using the most expensive care.
4. Patients have a lack of interest in lower cost care when they perceive—or assume—that the costs are borne by insurers and society, even if this includes depletion of scarce resources.

Source: Sommers, Dorr Gould, McGlunn, Pearson, and Danis (2013).

---

sufficiently robust metrics and variations in provider behavior such as gaming (Smith, 1995), it is evident that "quality report cards are here to stay" (Marshall, Shekelle, Davies, & Smith, 2003, p. 134). Yet some public quality reporting initiatives—for example, Medicare's public reporting initiative on hospital quality—have had little to no impact on mortality (Ryan, Nallamouthu, & Dimick, 2012). Other studies have found reporting-driven quality improvement in select settings, for example, nursing homes (Werner, Stuart, & Polsky, 2010) and outpatient diabetes clinics (Smith, Wright, Queram, & Lamb, 2012), to name but two. Still other studies have found puzzling relationships between quality goals and outcomes; for example, research by Fenton, Jerant, Bertakis, and Franks (2012) found an association between higher patient satisfaction and higher patient mortality. Finally, Laverty and colleagues (2012) note that British hospitals that have been publicly scrutinized for quality lapses did not experience decreased patient utilization in two of three hospitals and found only a short-term decrease in utilization of the third. Thus it could be suggested, based on this research, that public reporting of poor-quality outcomes did not deter patients from using the facility. These authors conclude that

> reporting designed to affect providers' reputations is likely to spur more improvement in quality and safety than relying on patients

to choose their providers based on quality and safety reports, and simplistic assumptions regarding the power of information to drive patient choice are unrealistic. (p. 593)

Nevertheless, the reporting of quality data, although in comparative infancy, gains additional prominence when more directly linked to payment such as in pay for performance (P4P) or accountable care organization shared savings programs (SSPs) that require quality targets to be met as a condition of enhanced payment in the case of P4P and saving in SSPs. For nurses, these approaches to payment introduce a much more complicated picture than what has traditionally been seen and identified as quality care and improvements. It requires an approach that uses a variety of analytic points and methodologies integrated to assess what constitutes quality. At the far extreme, it calls for analytic approaches reliant upon big data.

BIG DATA

An emerging area both within and beyond health care is the use of multiple data sets together to create a more nuanced understanding than could be gleaned by any one data set. Termed *big data*, such approaches have been used in industries outside of health care to decrease cost and increase quality, with Keenan (2014) sounding an urgent plea for *nursing big data*. But first, what is big data? Although a single unified definition of big data has not yet emerged, Roski, Bo-Linn, and Andrews (2014) note *the three Vs* characterizing big data as *volume, variety,* and *velocity*. Big data has massive amounts (volume) of data, potentially straining traditional data management systems. It uses many different data types (variety), which may range from diagnostic images to social media streaming and mobile applications, as well as structured and free text fields of electronic health records (EHRs). Thus, big data synthesizes and links divergent data sources to enable clinical, research, and policy questions to be answered in unprecedented ways (see Box 5.4 for examples). And finally, big data's massive data is processed rapidly (velocity). This velocity is a necessary element. Consider the case in which an accountable care organization wants to understand emergency department utilization by payer type in those with congestive heart failure, to see if additional care management is necessary for any one segment of their population. Data that are 2 years old would not be helpful. Taken as a whole, big data enables comprehensive analyses and discovery of patterns and potentials that could not be discerned with traditional methods and data sets.

Box 5.4

Potential Use of Big Data to Answer Clinical,
Research, and Policy Questions

Clinical Question: Are my patients actually filling their prescriptions?

Data Sources: Clinical data from an electronic health record (EHR) and insurance claims database. Linking the two would enable the provider to see not only what was prescribed but also what was filled, using submission to a payer as a proxy for filling the prescription. Note: Filling the prescription does not ensure that the patient is taking the medication, yet it provides more information than can be gleaned from EHRs only.

Research Question: What is the effect of various doses of aspirin on heart disease?

Data Sources: Insurance claims and EHR clinical data such as blood tests and medical histories. Note: This study is being conducted by the Patient-Centered Outcomes Research Institute, via a $10 million pilot study, with data from as many as 30 million people (Reardon, 2014).

Policy Question: Does mammography decrease death rate from breast cancer?

Data Sources: Statewide insurance claims databases linked over time with state vital record death statistics.

There are current limitations to the potential power of big data. It is estimated, for example, that less than 15% of EHR data is currently entered into a structured field enabling traditional analytic methods (Roski et al., 2014) and thus is lost to systematic individual and population health decision making and quality and cost review. Keenan (2014) makes the following troubling observation:

> What may shock most of our readers, is the fact that little to none of the data nurses [are] currently entering into EHRs can be used in the "big data" analysis. Unfortunately, all of that time spent checking pick-lists and entering narrative descriptions of one's nursing care has essentially yielded nursing data that are *not* analyzable. (emphasis in the original)

The transformative power of big data is yet to be fully understood, and it is essential that nurses begin to familiarize themselves with the concepts and applications. McKinsey Global Institute (Manyika et al., 2011) suggests that the use of big data in health care would offer a $300 billion/year of value to the U.S. health system in areas such as (a) comparative effectiveness research; (b) novel uses of clinical trial data for such things as predictive modeling; and (c) more personalized health care, based on an individual's personal health history, genomic profile, and lifestyle practices.

It should be noted, however, that at the time of this writing, the synthesis of claims data and clinical data is complex and challenges the capacity of most U.S. states that have been early adopters of these data systems and integration efforts. Moreover, there are important ethical considerations in the collection and use of the data, in particular in the area of privacy. Consider item (c) in the preceding paragraph. Such "personalized medicine" could potentially be crafted from data that includes all insurance claims, a genetic profile, data gained from personal social networking sites, and smart devices that record activity, sleep, and so on. Social media and software application data can provide deeply personal glimpses into patients' lives. Claims data, the full record of all treatment resulting in a claim to a payer, provide an unprecedented view of patient treatment over time. Data breaches in other sorts of data systems occur with enough regularity to suggest that caution is essential.

Who Has Access to Your Personal Health Data?

Different states have taken various routes to embrace the potential of big data and yet assure the level of privacy an individual desires. Let us look at insurance claims data as one example. Rhode Island allows individuals to opt out of inclusion in the state's all-payer claims database, whereas Vermont at the time of this writing is facing a legal challenge from a commercial insurer that is declining to provide claims data. Who is right? Should these data be collected and used for big data analyses?

Are the Ethics of Individual Privacy and Patient Autonomy at Odds With the Potential of Big Data?

Traditional health care ethics include a focus on patient autonomy and right to self-determination, suggesting that patients should have an easy way to opt out or to control what data are collected about them. This traditional health care ethics orientation has been reexamined by leading ethicists,

who have recently argued that patients have a moral obligation to participate as part of a common purpose to improve quality and decrease costs for
all (Faden et al., 2013). This offers yet another clear example of the tension
between individual-focused and population-focused perspectives in the contemporary era. Nevertheless, the era of big data in health care will persist,
and there is likely to be an acceleration of its use. The wise nurse will attend
to this development and expand his or her big data skill set.

MEANINGFUL USE

An additional element of the contemporary health care information area is
termed *meaningful use*. Meaningful use refers to using EHR technology in
particular ways, literally, to make EHR data meaningful (e.g., e-prescribing).
The overall objectives for the meaningful use initiative are (a) to improve
quality, safety, and efficiency and reduce health disparities; (b) to improve
care coordination and population and public health; and (c) to maintain
privacy and security of patient health information (Office of the National
Coordinator for Health Information Technology [n.d.]).

How, Why, and When Did the
Meaningful Use Initiative Start?

This meaningful use movement is rooted the American Reinvestment and
Recovery Act (ARRA) of 2009, which includes initiatives and funding to
modernize the U.S. health care infrastructure. The Health Information
Technology for Economic and Clinical Health (HITECH) Act supports the
development of EHRs and rewards providers who adopt meaningful use
criteria.

Are There Financial Incentives for
Meaningful Use Adoption?

Through *Medicare* and *Medicaid EHR Incentive Programs*, financial incentives
are used to reward eligible professionals and hospitals as they adopt, imple-
ment, upgrade, or demonstrate meaningful use of certified EHR technology.
Eligible professionals can receive up to $44,000 through the Medicare EHR
Incentive Program and up to $63,750 through the Medicaid EHR Incentive
Program and are thus incentivized to make this transition (Office of the
National Coordinator for Health Information Technology [n.d.]).

Meaningful Use Stages

The CMS administers this three-phased incentive program, scheduled to sunset in 2017. Stage one focuses on data capture and data sharing, stage two on advanced clinical processes, and stage three on improved outcomes. Take a moment to ask about the history of meaningful use efforts and outcomes in your clinical setting.

INFORMATION SCIENCE, QUALITY SCIENCE, AND DATA

What does the future hold for information science, quality science, data, and nursing? As health care cost concerns continue and the public feels more impact from seeking services due to cost sharing being more prevalent, it is likely that there will be accelerating attention to the value equation, that is, "What am I getting for my money?" Thus, it is likely that there will be increased attention on how valid information is defined, collected, and analyzed to determine the cost and value of health care. Increasingly sophisticated electronic medical record systems may link clinical information with financial information, such as the EHR–insurance claims data linkages illustrated in Box 5.4. Easily accessible quality data will enable patients and employer groups to quickly scan options for health care. In-home monitoring of a patient's health status provides yet a different form of information—patient-monitoring information—which could well revolutionize the nature of the patient–provider interaction. This chapter opened by illustrating the role of information in classic free markets, for example, the purchase of an appliance or coffee. It then detailed the historic challenges in "information" as it appears in health care markets, for example, asymmetry of information, and the phenomenon of supplier-induced demand. The role of data in discerning value, both cost and outcomes, was described, including emerging trends such as big data. In health care, the information revolution is just beginning. The savvy nurse understands the role of information in accountability for both cost and outcomes, continually expands skills to use complex data sources in clinical practice, and embraces a spirit of adventure in exploring new technological applications.

Thought Questions

1. Recall your first cell phone or the oldest cell phone you have seen. Then reflect on the most up-to-date phone you have seen. What features do you notice on the new phone? These features can be called functionalities. Now, describe health care cost and quality information you have seen. Has it been helpful? What functionalities would add additional value to your use of your personal health data? What functionalities do you use in clinical practice? What aspects are useful and which would benefit from enhancement?

2. Your neighbor is considering an elective surgery and notices that the available price information suggests that the procedure is nearly three times as expensive in Setting A than Setting B. The neighbor then asks you what to do. What other information is needed to make a recommendation to your neighbor? Do considerations change if your neighbor has a low-deductible plan versus a high-deductible plan?

3. What sorts of data would be useful to planning care strategies for a selected population of patients? How does planning for the population differ from planning for the individual? What sorts of data are useful for both individual and population approaches?

4. What knowledge and skills prepare you to understand and apply big data in clinically relevant ways? What additional skills are needed?

5. Define the following key terms:

   Asymmetry of information

   Big data

   Informed decision making

   Meaningful use

   Price transparency

   Price variability

Exercises

1. Describe ways you have seen information used in the health care system. What recommendations would you offer to improve the flow and accuracy of health information?

2. Prepare a presentation for your peers that provides information on how to talk to patients about the cost of care within a framework of quality and overall value. Include opportunities for role-playing.

Quiz

TRUE OR FALSE

1. One characteristic of a classic free market is that the consumer knows about the product or, alternatively, how to obtain information about the product.

2. The term price transparency refers to the degree to which the price of a product or service is readily evident.

3. The same health care service provided by different providers always costs the patient the exact same amount.

4. A weakness of shared decision making models is the exclusion of patients' values and wishes when planning a therapeutic approach to their care.

5. Health care data and the use of quality metrics consistently improve the quality of care while decreasing cost.

6. High patient satisfaction has consistently been associated with high-quality patient outcomes.

7. *Big data* is characterized by volume, variety, and velocity.

8. In health care, the term *meaningful use* refers to the usefulness of websites for access to health insurance information.

9. One potential use of big data is to address clinical, research, and policy questions.

10. One ethical consideration in the use of patients' personal health information in big data analyses is the protection of patient privacy.

MULTIPLE CHOICE

11. Barriers to considering cost in shared decision making between providers and patients include
   A. Patients may perceive the most expensive care as the best care
   B. Patients and providers are skilled in discussing cost within the context of health care
   C. Both A and B
   D. Neither A nor B

12. Shared decision making is
   A. A provision of the Affordable Care Act
   B. Defined as a collaborative process that allows patients and their provider to make health decisions together
   C. Both A and B
   D. Neither A nor B

13. The use of quality metrics and measurement targets for reimbursement is an element of
   A. Fee-for-service reimbursement
   B. Accountable care shared savings programs
   C. Both A and B
   D. Neither A nor B

14. Big data
   A. Enables comprehensive analyses and discovery of patterns that could not be discerned with a single data set
   B. Consistently includes nursing data entries
   C. Both A and B
   D. Neither A nor B

15. Potentially, big data can support
   A. Comparative effectiveness research
   B. Personalized health care
   C. Both A and B
   D. Neither A nor B

REFERENCES

Arrow, K. (1963). Uncertainty and the welfare economics of medical care. *American Economic Review, 53*(5), 141–149.

Bodenheimer, T., & Grumbach, K. (2012). *Understanding health policy: A clinical approach.* New York, NY: McGraw Hill/Lang.

Dartmouth Atlas of Health Care. (n.d.) *Understanding of the efficiency and effectiveness of the health care system.* Retrieved September 10, 2014, from http://www.dartmouthatlas.org

Dentzer, S. (2013, May 21). Sorting out the meaning of hospital pricing disparities [Blog post]. Retrieved March 5, 2014, from http://www.rwjf.org/en/blogs/culture-of-health/2013/05/sorting_out_the_mean.html

EHR Incentive Programs. (n.d). Retreived February 23, 2015 from www.healthit.gov/providers-professionals/ehr-incentive-programs

Faden, R., Kass, N., Goodman, S., Pronovost, P., Tunis, S., & Beauchamp, T. (2013). An ethics framework for a learning health care system: A departure from traditional research ethics and clinical ethics. *Ethical Oversight of Learning Health Care Systems, Hastings Center Report Special Report, 43*(1), S16–S27. doi:10.1002/hast.134

Fenton, J. J., Jerant, A. F., Bertakis, K. D., & Franks, P. (2012). The cost of satisfaction. *Archives of Internal Medicine, 172*, 405–411.

Ginsburg, P. (2010, November). *Wide variation in hospital and physician payment rates evidence of provider market power* (Research Brief No. 16). Washington, DC: Center for Studying Health Systems Change.

Informed Medical Decisions Foundation. *Advancing shared decision making.* Retrieved September 10, 2014, from www.informedmedicaldecisions.org

Keenan, G. (2014). Big data in health care: An urgent mandate to CHANGE nursing EHRs! *Online Journal of Nursing Informatics (OJNI), 18*(1). Retrieved from http://ojni.org/issues/?p=3081

Laverty, A., Smith, P., Pape, U., Mears, A., Wachter, R., & Millett, C. (2012). High-profile investigations into hospital safety problems in England did not prompt patients to switch providers. *Health Affairs, 31*(3), 593–601. doi:10.1377/hlthaff.2011.0810

Lee, E., & Emanuel, E. (2013). Shared decision making to improve care and reduce cost. *New England Journal of Medicine, 368*(1), 6–8. doi:10.1056/NEJMp1209500

Manyika, J., Chui, M., Brown, B., Bughin, J., Dobbs, R., Roxburgh, C. & Byers, A. (2011). *Big data: The next frontier for innovation, competition, and productivity.* Washington, DC: McKinsey Global Institute.

Marshall, M. N., Shekelle, P. G., Davies, H. T. O., & Smith, P. C. (2003). Public reporting on quality in the United States and the United Kingdom [editor's prologue]. *Health Affairs, 22*(3), 134–148.

Mayes, R. (2007). The origins, development, and passage of Medicare's revolutionary prospective payment system. *Journal of the History of Medicine and Allied Sciences, 62*(1), 21–55. doi:10.1093/jhmas/jrj038

Mullan, F., & Wennberg, J. (2004). Wrestling with variation: An interview with Jack Wennberg. *Health Affairs, 1*, VAR 73–VAR 80. doi:10.1377/hlthaff.var.73

Mulley, A. (2009). Inconvenient truths about supplier induced demand and unwarranted variation in medical practice. *British Medical Journal, 339*, b4073.

Office of the National Coordinator for Health Information Technology. (n.d.). *EHR Incentive Programs.* Retrieved February 23, 2015, from http://www.healthit.gov/providers oprofessionals/ehr-incentive-programs

Reardon, S. (2014). US big-data health network launches aspirin study. *Nature, 512*(7512), 18.

Roski, J., Bo-Linn, G., & Andrews, T. (2014). Creating value in health care through big data: Opportunities and policy implications. *Health Affairs, 33*(7), 1115–1122.

Ryan, A., Nallamouthu, B., & Dimick, J. (2012). Medicare's public reporting initiative on hospital quality had modest or no impact on mortality from three key conditions. *Health Affairs, 31*, 585–592.

Smith, M., Wright, A., Queram, C., & Lamb, G. (2012). Public reporting helped drive quality improvements in outpatient diabetes care among Wisconsin physician groups. *Health Affairs, 31*, 570–570. doi:10.1377/hlthaff.2012.0686

Smith, P. (1995). On the unintended consequences of publishing performance data in the public sector. *International Journal of Public Administration, 18*(2–3), 277–310.

Sommers, R., Dorr Gould, S., McGlunn, E., Pearson, S., & Danis, M. (2013). Focus groups highlight that many patients object to clinicians' focusing on costs. *Health Affairs, 32*, 338–346.

Werner, R., Stuart, E., & Polsky, D. (2010). Public reporting drove quality gains at nursing homes. *Health Affairs, 29*, 1706–1710.

6

MARKET ENTRY, EXIT, AND ANTITRUST LAW

CHAPTERS 4 AND 5 detailed two key ways in which health care markets differ from classic free markets, as an organizing framework for understanding health care economics as well as to illuminate emerging health care trends. These first two principles—(a) buyers bear the consequences of their decision making; and (b) buyers have information about the product, or know how to obtain information—are complemented by two additional principles: (c) Sellers are free to enter and exit the market; and (d) no one buyer or seller is large enough to influence the market. Chapter 6 now details these two additional ways in which health care markets differ from classic free markets, to further explicate contemporary issues in health care reform. Recall, however, that the goal of the comparison between health care and classic free markets is to illuminate complex issues rather than to suggest that health care markets can or should function like classic free markets.

Following completion of this chapter, you will be able to

- Explain the rationale for Certificate of Need (CON) legislation
- Describe basic elements of antitrust law
- Consider the impact of antitrust law on health care and the role of the nurse

ENTERING AND EXITING THE MARKET

Sharon has always enjoyed baking. Typically, she uses the finest ingredients—real butter, rich cream, the finest chocolate. Inheriting a bit of money after her father died, Sharon decides to open a small bakery, specializing in traditional Italian and German pastries. After an initially rocky start and nearly losing all of her start-up capital, Germalian, as she named her bakery, was doing fairly well. The 12-hour workdays notwithstanding, Sharon was enjoying her work and her life as an entrepreneur. Near the end of her third year in business, Sharon was dismayed to learn that Big Company Health Food Store was opening just up the block from her bakery. Big Company not only includes a high-end bakery, they also have a coffee shop where customers can sample and enjoy the baked goods...and almost always buy something to take home. Sharon notes that Big Company's high-end pastries are less expensive than hers... much less expensive, and they also have a middle-of-the-line set of baked products. As a large chain, Big Company benefits from lower cost of ingredients due to bulk buying. Also, with over 149 stores in all states, they can simply undercut Sharon on cost until she loses her market share. Sharon contemplates using less expensive ingredients, or smaller portions to compete on price, but also worries she will then lose on quality. She tries both strategies. Nevertheless, in less than a year after Big Company opened, Sharon was bankrupt, having lost all of her initial investment and most of her savings.

In this example, Sharon was free to enter the market. So was Big Company. In classic free markets, companies compete with each other on the basis of price, quality, and public demand. Consumers "decide with their feet," purchasing what they want and when and where they want it. Businesses must meet zoning and safety regulations. They also must come up with the capital—the funds to start the business—either through personal money, loans, or some other mechanism. With exceptions (for example, regulations to limit the density of liquor establishments or other issues for public safety), entry into the market is typically not rigidly regulated. Such *laissez-faire* enterprise is guided by an overall doctrine that opposes governmental interference or oversight and is characterized by a conscious, deliberate absence of governmental involvement beyond that necessary for peace, property rights, and public safety. Individual are free to enter the market, but also—as in Sharon's case when her business could not withstand the competition from Big Company—to exit. While Sharon was perfectly free to enter the market, she was also, unfortunately for her, free to fail.

How Are Health Care Markets Different From This Example?

In a typical health care case, providers do not raise the capital for their enterprise, nor are they personally financially liable for financial failure. A group of physicians who wish to use robotic-assisted surgery, for example, do not raise the money for the purchase of the equipment that will enable them to charge for new services and potentially charge more for the service than the service it is replacing. Instead, the hospital purchases the equipment, the cost of which is diffusely passed on to the consumer in the form of higher hospital rates and correspondingly higher insurance rate. Thus, some of the typical market checks are not in place. Recall also the phenomenon of supplier-induced demand described in the previous two chapters. The purchase of a new piece of equipment means some demand for that equipment will be created, even if care outcomes would be the same without it.

Are Health Care Organizations Free to Fail or Exit the Market?

Some health care organizations that would not be financially viable under typical free market principles and practices are subsidized or differently reimbursed to ensure that they do not exit the market. Examples include critical access hospitals, discussed in Chapter 9, and *federally qualified health centers*. Federally qualified health centers receive enhanced reimbursement from Medicare and Medicaid and must serve an underserved population or area. Other examples of subsidies to help prop up care delivery that may not be financially viable without that extra help are *disproportionate share* subsidies to organizations that treat a higher proportion of Medicare or Medicaid patients.

What About Freedom to Enter the Market?

In an effort to better align health care investments with societal need, *Certificate of Need* (CON) legislation was passed, and CON programs were implemented to restrain growth of facilities and the cost of such growth. A second goal of CON legislation is to better coordinate new construction and services, rather than allowing new constructions and services to develop unchecked. Initially developed on a state-by-state basis, the 1974 *Health*

Planning Resources Development Act required all states to have processes by which all capital projects—for example, the purchase of high-tech equipment or the construction of new buildings—would be reviewed and approval required before any action to purchase or construct was taken. In theory, purchase or construction that did not meet true societal need would not be approved. Adoption of this approach was incentivized with federal funding, yet both the Act and the funding were repealed in 1987. Modifications to state CON laws then proceeded on a state-by-state basis, with some states rescinding the CON process and others retaining CON. As of the time of this writing, 36 states retain some sort of CON, although the exact provisions and *threshold triggers* differ by state. The term threshold trigger refers to the conditions or situations that set off a CON review. For example, in one state, Michigan, community need must be documented for all purchases regardless of cost, while in others, such as South Carolina, there is no review of projects below a certain cost. Still other states have CON only for particular elements of the health care industry, for example, long-term care. Review and approval are needed to build a new hospital in all states with CON laws (National Council of State Legislatures, 2014).

DOES CON WORK?

Perceptions of the effectiveness of CON vary, with some analyses finding the process to be more influenced by politics than policy (Yee, Stark, Bond, & Carrier, 2011). Another study concludes that the CON process helped prevent duplication of services in the scenarios they analyzed (Lucas, Siewers, Goodman, Wang, & Wennberg, 2011).

CON AND PAYMENT REFORM

Payment reform is also impacting both market entry of new postacute (after hospital) services as well as market exit, with evidence to date suggesting that fewer new services are entering the marketplace and exits are increasing (Huckfeldt, Sood, Romley, Malchiodi, & Escarce, 2013). The extent to which new payment models that embrace provider risk sharing modify or replace CON intentions is unclear. Recall, for example, the payment reform models described in Chapter 3. In a fee-for-service environment, new equipment can catalyze a demand for new services and create new revenue for the hospital, even though this action represents an overall cost to society. Would a hospital under a global budget be more prudent about expansion of services or creation of new buildings? Likely, as these are the very sorts of incentives global budgets are designed to create. Thus, the evolution, application, and usefulness of CON laws in a reformed payment environment are unclear at this time.

Licensing Laws

CON programs are one way that health care markets differ from classic free markets. Licensing laws are another. A professional license is a form of monopoly on services; an RN, for example, cannot legally offer physical therapy services. Although licenses provide some level of information about what a provider can do and what a patient can expect, the monopolist power of organized medicine is associated with difficulty containing cost. To illustrate this complex idea, ponder, for example, if when the first McDonald's restaurant opened, they had a situation similar to medicine's scope of practice in which no other entity could sell hamburgers. Such monopolies are not allowed in free markets, and competition among different hamburger sellers helps to control cost and spur innovation and quality. Group and Roberts (2001) argue that physicians have created that monopoly in part through the subordination of nurses, who could provide a legitimate, quality-enhancing form of competition—a perspective that has some powerful allies, which is the focus of the next section.

NURSES AND THE MONOPOLISTIC POWER OF MEDICAL LICENSES

The regulation of advanced practice nurses pointedly illustrates the dilemma of unnecessary restriction of nurses' scope of practice. Renowned health economist Uwe Reinhardt (cited in Henderson, 2013) notes:

> Organized medicine invariably opposes wider scopes of practice and independent practice of nonphysician health professionals, ostensibly not to protect economic turf but to protect the quality of patient care. Curiously, one rarely finds those to be protected by this paternalism vocally on organized medicine's side.
>
> Not many economists today are buying the medical profession's position on this issue. More typically, economists lean toward [Milton] Friedman's more cynical view. They regard professional licensure of any kind—almost always proposed by the very professionals or occupations to be licensed—mainly as a means to endow the licensees with monopolistic market power.

Although progress has been made, physicians retain control of nurse practitioners (NPs) in many U.S. states, despite consistent evidence of NPs' quality and cost effectiveness. Indeed, staff of the powerful Federal Trade Commission (FTC, 2014), which exists to promote market competition to enhance quality, urges states to remove barriers to NP practice, stating:

> Physician supervision requirements may raise competition concerns because they effectively give one group of health care professionals the ability to restrict access to the market by another, competing group of health care professionals, thereby denying health care consumers the benefits of greater competition. In addition, APRNs [advanced practice registered nurses] play a critical role in alleviating provider shortages and expanding access to health care services for medically underserved populations. For these reasons, the FTC staff has consistently urged state legislators to avoid imposing restrictions on APRN scope of practice unless those restrictions are necessary to address well-founded patient safety concerns. Based on substantial evidence and experience, expert bodies have concluded that ARPNs are safe and effective as independent providers of many health care services within the scope of their training, licensure, certification, and current practice. Therefore, new or extended layers of mandatory physician supervision may not be justified. (pp. 1–2)

Thus, the manner in which classic free markets continually refine cost and quality—through high-value products and services gaining market share while low-value products lose market share—is dramatically altered in health care. Removal of barriers that prevent nurses and NPs from functioning within their full scope of practice is one valuable step toward quality enhancement within an environment of cost containment.

MERGE, CONSOLIDATE, OR STAND ALONE: AN OVERVIEW OF ANTITRUST LAW

U.S. *antitrust law* was created to ensure that no one buyer or seller is large enough to dominate the market, the monopolistic tendency noted earlier. Rooted in concerns about potentially monopolist control of key industries in the late 1800s, the foundational Sherman Antitrust Act of 1880 protects competition by making it illegal to restrain free trade. Augmented by amendments and additional laws such as the Clayton Antitrust Act of 1914, the fundamental principle behind antitrust law is to support market competition as a means to enhance quality, contain costs, and—importantly—drive innovation. As Kesselheim and Shiu (2013) note: "Antitrust law limits anti-competitive behavior that prevents the free market from rewarding the true winner." The heretofore-mentioned Federal Trade Commission serves as the nation's antitrust watchdog.

Application of antitrust law to health care is complex and multifaceted, and full explication is beyond the scope of this text. However, nurses need to understand the threats to positive competition and the basic rationale behind contemporary antitrust issues. Dafny (2014), for example, notes that health reform efforts, specifically the Affordable Care Act, "unleashed a merger frenzy, with hospitals scrambling to shore up their market positions, improve operational efficiency, and create organizations capable of managing population health" (p. 198). At the same time, evidence supporting positive societal impact and related outcomes from such mergers is scant. Gaynor and Town (2012) examined hospital consolidations and report that

1. Hospital market consolidation increases the cost of care—costs which in turn are passed on to citizens in the form of higher insurance premiums, fewer benefits, and lower wages.
2. Hospital competition is associated with increased quality.
3. Physician–hospital consolidation has not led to an increase in quality or to a decrease in cost.

Moreover, when physicians move from being independent physicians to become hospital-employed physicians, the charge to the consumer is higher for the same services due to the additional billing of *facility fees* associated with hospital-employed physician practices even if that physician remains in the same outpatient setting. The cost impact may extend beyond ambulatory visits; Baker, Bundorf, and Kessler (2014) found higher hospital prices and spending in markets where hospitals had ownership of physician practices.

IS CONSOLIDATION THE SAME AS INTEGRATION?

The terms *consolidation* and *integration* are often loosely applied. In general, providers of a similar type under a common organizational structure reflect *vertical integration*, while providers of different service types, such as hospitals, nursing homes, and home health care agencies within a common organizational structure, reflect *horizontal integration*. Although termed integration, there is an important distinction between consolidation and actual integration, regardless of the terms used. Consolidation is simply bringing together two (or more) previously independent entities. Integration instead implies a synthesis or redesign that eliminates "unnecessary duplication" and creates a "comprehensive management of the organization as a whole" (Gaynor & Town, 2012, p. 3). Such comprehensive management of the whole offers nurses the opportunity to seize a leadership role in the creation of a new paradigm of more comprehensive, integrated care. Continuing old models of care delivery, merely aggregated to increase market power, have not consistently demonstrated the transformation needed for broad societal impact. Nurses can play a key role in creating truly integrated systems.

Thought Questions

1. Why do some states retain Certificate of Need regulation and others do not?

2. Using an economic and market perspective, how would you argue for removal of state restrictions that stop nurses from practicing to the full extent of their preparation?

3. Define the following key terms:

   Antitrust law

   Certificate of Need

   Consolidation versus integration

   Facility fee

   Federally qualified health center

   Horizontal integration

   Vertical integration

Exercise

1. Prepare a list of hospitals or health systems that have recently reorganized in your area. What patterns do you see? What forces served as an impetus? What has been the impact on nursing? What has been the impact on the patient experience?

Quiz

TRUE OR FALSE

1. Disproportionate share subsidies are provided to some health care organizations that treat a high proportion of individuals with commercial insurance.

2. Medical licenses are a form of monopoly.

3. In 2014, the U.S. Federal Trade Commission staff published a report critical of states' restriction of nurse practitioner scope of practice because it is an inappropriate restraint of appropriate market competition.

4. The passage of the Affordable Care Act has led to mergers among hospitals and other health care organizations.

5. When an independent physician becomes a hospital-employed physician, the charge for that physician's care may be higher due to the inclusion of an additional facility fee.

6. Antitrust law exists to assure that no one buyer or seller is large enough to dominate the market and therefore disable the potential for market competition.

7. Integration of health services, unlike consolidation, redesigns care delivery to eliminate unnecessary duplication.

8. In health care, some facilities that would not be financially viable are subsidized to prevent their exit from the marketplace.

MULTIPLE CHOICE

9. Certificate of Need legislation
   A. Attempts to restrain unnecessary growth of health care facilities
   B. Has been rescinded in all U.S. states, to comply with provisions in the Affordable Care Act
   C. Both A and B
   D. Neither A nor B

10. Hospital consolidations
    A. Have consistently decreased the cost of health care
    B. Have decreased competition among hospitals and as a result increased quality of care
    C. Both A and B
    D. Neither A nor B

11. Federally qualified health centers
    A. Receive enhanced reimbursement from Medicare and Medicaid
    B. Must serve an otherwise underserved population
    C. Both A and B
    D. Neither A nor B

12. In a classic free market, buyers and sellers are free to
    A. Enter the marketplace
    B. Exit the marketplace
    C. Both A and B
    D. Neither A nor B

REFERENCES

Baker, L., Bundorf, M., & Kessler, D. (2014). Vertical integration: Hospital ownership of physician practices is associated with higher prices and spending. *Health Affairs, 33*(5), 756–765.

Dafny, L. (2014). Hospital industry consolidation—still more to come? *New England Journal of Medicine, 370*(3), 198–199. doi:10.1056/NEJMp1313948

Federal Trade Commission. (2014). *Policy perspectives: Competition and the regulation of advanced practice nurses.* Washington, DC: Author.

Gaynor, M., & Town, R. (2012). The impact of hospital consolidation—update. *The synthesis project* (Policy Brief No. #9). Princeton, NJ: The Robert Wood Johnson Foundation.

Group, T., & Roberts, J. (2001). *Nursing, physician control, and the medical monopoly: Historical perspectives on gender inequality in roles, rights, and range of practice.* Bloomington, IN: Indiana University Press.

Henderson, D. (2013, October 17). Reinhardt on doctor's monopoly. *Library of Economics and Liberty.* Retrieved March 23, 2014, from http://econlog.econlib .org/archives/2013/10/reinhardt_on_do.html

Huckfeldt, P., Sood, N., Romley, J., Malchiodi, A., & Escarce, J. (2013). Medicare payment reform and provider entry and exit in the post-acute care market. *Health Services Research, 48*(5), 1557–1580.

Kesselheim, A., & Shiu, N. (2013). *FTC v. Actavis: The Supreme Court issues a reversal on reverse payments.* Retrieved March 24, 2014, from http://healthaffairs .org/blog/2013/06/21/ftc-v-actavis-the-supreme-court-issues-a-reversal-on-reverse-payments

Lucas, F., Siewers, A., Goodman, D., Wang, D., & Wennberg, D. (2011). New cardiac surgery programs established from 1993 to 2004 led to little increased access, substantial duplication of services. *Health Affairs, 30*(8), 1569–1574. doi:10.1377/hlthaff.2010.0210

National Conference of State Legislatures. (2014). Certificate of need: State health laws and programs. Retrieved March 17, 2014, from http://www.ncsl.org/research/health/con-certificate-of-need-state-laws.aspx

Yee, T., Stark, L., Bond, A., & Carrier, E. (2011). Health care certificate-of-need laws: Policy or politics? *National Institute for Health Care Reform* (Issues Brief No. 4). Washington, DC: National Institute for Health Care Reform.

ETHICS AND ECONOMICS IN AN AGE OF REFORM

U nlike you, individuals who are not aware of the cost and harm of over-treatment may consider ensuring a lot of treatment to be the most ethical approach to health reform efforts. Many nurses and other providers see the flaws in the current system, but do not have the background in health economics that enables them to dissect the issues, consider the ethical implications, and use moral reasoning to create better systems of care and a better society. You now have that background. The first two sections of this text have provided the foundation that now enables us to layer on yet another important dimension of finance, economics, and policy in an age of reform: ethics.

Chapter 7 presents an orientation in which ethics and economics are not at odds, but merely different sides of the same coin. This orientation is purposely chosen to counter the notion that considerations of economics are bad or unethical in health care, rather than essential to both individual patients and to society at large.

Chapter 8 then reviews different models for ethical decision making that you can use in daily practice as well as in broader systems redesign and reform efforts.

Let us start first with Chapter 7, to ensure that you can lace together ethical and economic considerations in your decision-making actions and inactions.

WHAT IS ETHINOMICS?

FOLLOWING COMPLETION OF this chapter, you will be able to

- Describe classic principles of health care ethics
- Consider the relationship between individually focused ethical perspectives and population-based perspectives
- Detail the relationship between health care ethics and health care economics

> *Peter, a high school senior, is not sure what he wants to study in college. He enjoys science and math and considers a career in engineering. Pondering his favorite playtime activities at age 5, playing superhero, Peter recalls that what he has most wanted to do is to "do good"...to help. Peter decides to look more closely at a nursing career.*

CAN ECONOMICS COEXIST WITH THE INTENTION OF "DOING GOOD"?

The intention of doing good, or *beneficence*, is not only central to professional nursing's code of ethics, but also at the heart of the attraction of many nurses to the profession in the first place. Avoidance of doing harm, known as *non-maleficence*, is the obverse principle of health care ethics rooted in the wisdom of the ancient Greek physician Hippocrates, who said, "Above all else, do no harm." For many nurses, "doing good" and "not harming" seem like simple, uncomplicated responsibilities with easily aligned tasks; you do what you can for the patient before you, working hard to avoid errors or mistakes. Certainly, one might argue, none of these should seem constrained by issues of economics. Such a view, however, belies the complexity of ethical decision making and also incorrectly suggests that economics is a counterforce to ethics. The premise underlying this chapter is that ethics and economics are different faces of the same coin. Moreover, health providers often feel more comfortable articulating the principles of ethics than economics or may actually be uneasy with either. Yet both are foundational nursing knowledge in the age of reform.

Schaller (2008) notes that many issues are shaped by the underlying economics of the situation, yet Americans are not willing to speak about economic realities because to do so appears to dehumanize people. Schaller states:

> In reality, public policy decisions that are made legitimately for economic reasons are often clothed in other garb.... [I]t is not uncommon for vital economic concerns that actually drive the dispute to be unspoken and unacknowledged.... It would be far better for the underlying backgrounds to be openly disclosed and discussed during the policy debate rather than concealed. (p. 4)

It is essential that vital concerns rooted in economic realities be openly disclosed and discussed. Consistently ranked as America's most trusted professionals (Gallup, 2013), nurses have a key opportunity to lead the articulation of ethics and economics in health care.

Ethinomics

Medical ethicist Merrill Mathews suggests that the term *ethinomics* can be used to describe the area in which economics and ethics converge in public policy (Mathews, 1999). This notion is useful because it reflects the conjoined nature of economic and ethical issues as different sides of the same coin and invites both underlying elements to be open to public debate in policy formation. Such an orientation offers valuable tools for the nurse and offers a conceptual orientation that holds both economics and ethics in the forefront. This is a fresh and new perspective. Indeed, principles of health care ethics historically have not brought the economic impact of decision making into focus. Instead, the *universal principles of health care ethics* have focused on care of the individual, with little attention to the impact of clinical decision making on overall population health. Moreover, although universal principles have guided practice, they can conflict with each other in actual application. A therapy, for example, may be prescribed to benefit a patient, but instead result in harm, and thus, beneficence and nonmaleficence are in conflict. Moreover, conflict can exist between autonomy—the patient's right to informed choice—and nonmaleficence, and each of these with population-based justice.

> Mr. Greenfield has recently been diagnosed with colon cancer. His surgeon is pleased with how well Mr. Greenfield, at age 86, tolerated the surgery. One small node was found, but Dr. Knife is confident that Mr. Greenfield will die with the cancer rather than of it. He talks to Mr. Greenfield, suggesting no further treatment. Mr. Greenfield, however, seems reluctant to forgo more treatment. He states that chemotherapy might be a good idea because "everyone needs a good flushing out once in a while." Dr. Knife laughs, stating, "This isn't an enema, Mr. Greenfield, it is chemotherapy." Mr. Greenfield is insistent, however, and is not willing to hear about the potential risks in relation to benefits of chemotherapy for this particular type of cancer at his age. Finally, Dr. Knife reluctantly orders an oncology consult. As the patient walks out the door, Dr. Knife mutters to himself, "I know where this will go." Mr. Greenfield starts chemotherapy a week later.

In the United States, the principle of autonomy has been applied in a manner that reflects an individual's right to make her or his own decisions. In practice, it often trumps other principles. Dr. Knife is legitimately concerned that chemotherapy will not help Mr. Greenfield and instead has great potential to do harm. In this scenario, autonomy is in direct conflict with beneficence and nonmaleficence. Note that cost is not part of this decision, yet the cost—financial, emotional, and social—is real. Overtreatment of Mr. Greenfield—treatment that is unlikely to help—harms not only Mr. Greenfield, but also society at large because the resources used in his care are not available for other societal needs. Recall that health care is largely paid for through taxes (Medicare and Medicaid), and employees with commercial insurance functioning as a reduction in real wages forming a hidden tax. Historically, the ethical decision making lens has focused on maximizing the care of the individual without consideration of the broader implications of the cumulative impact of clinical decisions on the population at large or over time. This tension between individual autonomy and the overall population good is not easily visible to providers seeing patients in a clinical setting. Eddy (1996) states:

Well intentioned attempts to maximize the care of individual patients can harm other people. The sense of harm is lessened by depersonalizing these other people and seeing them only through statistics. But in reality, they are just as real as the individual patients we see face to face. (pp. 109–110)

At the same time, such maximization of care, even without benefit, has been enormously lucrative to providers. Providers have viewed their accountability as being limited to the person right in front of them, largely blinded to the impact on others in society (horizontal effects) and impacts over intergenerational time (temporal or longitudinal effects). As such, the accountability horizon for clinical decision making in fee-for-service systems has not served society well. Newacheck and Benjamin (2004), for example, argue that *entitlement funding* for Medicare, health care that you are "entitled to" simply because you are over 65, differentially places societal resources in the hands of the elderly at the expense of younger generations and thus represents intergenerational injustice. Providers such as Dr. Knife, as well as the oncologist and oncology nurses later treating Mr. Greenfield, do not see themselves as violating principles of justice and fairness; they are simply doing the work before them. Nevertheless, seen or unseen, overtreatment does remove finances from the pool of resources potentially available to treat others. Professional accountability horizons have simply been too narrow and short term to account for these broader effects of clinical decision making. The time and resources the oncology nurse and oncologist devote to Mr. Greenfield, for example, do take treatment resources away from another patient who could really benefit and raises the cost of care for all. The shift from fee-for-service to population-based global budgets or bundled payments discussed in earlier chapters begins to better align these overlapping responsibilities.

SOCIAL DETERMINANTS OF HEALTH, HEALTH DISPARITIES, ETHICS, AND ECONOMICS

The intersection of economics and the ethics of societal good can also be understood from the perspective of social determinants of health. Although an enormous amount of the nation's resources goes into medical care, this care makes a relatively small contribution to the overall health status (see Figure 1.1), with the best predictor of health status being lifestyle and the environment, both of which are affected by socioeconomic status (SES). Adler and Newman (2002) note, "The most fundamental causes of health disparities are socioeconomic disparities" (p. 61). SES, although not identical to, is well correlated with educational attainment. Thus, it might be argued that to enhance *health*, resources now used for *health care* might be redirected to education to defray the cost of college and reduce student debt load (another national goal), given that—in general—the better the education of the person, the better the health status. As Adler and Newman note:

> Education is perhaps the most basic SES component since it shapes future occupational opportunities and earning potential. It also provides knowledge and life skills that allow better-educated persons to gain more ready access to information and resources to promote health... . To the extent that education is key to health inequalities, policies encouraging more years of schooling and supporting early childhood education may have health benefits... . When policy makers debate the merits of increasing access to education, they rarely consider improvement in the health of the population...collateral benefits such as decreasing health care costs also might emerge from increasing investment in education. (pp. 61–62)

Similarly, excessive resources put into health care could be redirected to the sort of job creation that can enhance the SES of individuals and their families. These sorts of policy trade-offs are not always fully visible to the nurse or the general public, but are trade-offs nonetheless. Thus, as an informed nurse, you can more broadly consider the impact of your work, including the impacts of overtreatment, and understand it as an ethical issue with broad impact.

Much of the increase in life expectancy over the past century is due to improvements in living conditions and a reduction in overcrowding, as well as reduction in deaths from infectious disease. The former represents a standard-of-living issue, not a health care issue, and the latter, a public health initiative. In the United States, health expenditures in 2013 reached $2.9 trillion, or 17.4% of the gross domestic product (CMS.gov, 2012). This means that of all the money spent on goods and services in the United States, 17 cents on every dollar goes into health care; hence, those dollars are not available for other goods and services like education, housing, entertainment, and childcare. Arguably, overtreatment harms individuals and society and therefore violates principles of health care ethics.

Ethinomics, Autonomy, and Justice

Ethinomics is concerned with such issues. It recognizes that economic forces interact with principles like autonomy and intergenerational justice. Should Mr. Greenfield, for example, be able to have any services he wishes, particularly given that although he paid taxes into Medicare, others are also paying for these services through their taxes? Or should there be limits on what Mr. Greenfield can demand? If so, who should define those limits? When do autonomy and right to self-determination become illogical and damaging? An emphasis on the wishes of the individual as a primary determinant of what constitutes perceived ethical conduct is a distinctive part of contemporary U.S. culture, but is not universal.

> *Sylvain, a Canadian, is chatting with Paula, an American, regarding public testing for HIV/AIDS. Paula believes that everyone who is sexually active should be tested. After all, she reasons, the test is free through the public health clinic. Sylvain is bewildered. "HIV/AIDS testing is expensive, Paula, and it needs to be done in a thoughtful, strategic, and focused manner," he states. Who is correct?*

Paula and Sylvain are simply looking at this issue at different levels, and at different levels of comprehensiveness. Paula perceives that HIV/AIDS testing is free simply because *she* can get it for free. Paula is failing to look at the overall costs. The test is not free. In a publicly funded clinic, the costs of the test are picked up by the public through taxes. Sylvain, reared in a very different health system and culture, is aware that the test is expensive even though the test—like all of his health care—does not include an out-of-pocket charge at the time of the visit.

The issue of where the cost is borne along the scale from individual to society at large is only one end of the continuum. The other issue addresses this question: "Who benefits financially?" In health care, one person's or group's cost is another's gain.

> *George Jones, chief executive officer (CEO) of Cityville Hospital, is pleased! The hospital has had a banner year. Revenues are have shot through the roof in almost every service line. Surgical revenues were up 9%, medical revenues up 4%, and emergency service revenues up a whopping 12%. CEO Jones is excited that the hospital just may finally be creating the financial reserves needed to undertake a highly anticipated capital project, a new entrance to the emergency department. He also thinks they can bump the nursing salary pool increase an additional 0.5% from the level requested by the union. He excitedly calls Cityville's chief nursing officer, Floyd Boyd, to share the good news.*

Jennifer Boyd, CEO of a large company in Cityville, is perplexed and worried. As a large employer, she has been able to negotiate lower insurance rates for her employees, through a preferred provider arrangement that requires employees to use Cityville Hospital or pay large out-of-pocket copayments and coinsurance. Because the insurance pool is so large, the financial expense of any one employee has been spread over many people. This risk sharing over such a large group, coupled with the discounted rates she was able to negotiate with Cityville Hospital in exchange for the arrangement in which her employees use Cityville service only, has meant the lowest insurance premium in the region! Jennifer knows this has been one of the reasons she has been able to attract such a talented workforce. Now her human resources director shares this information: "Employee utilization of health care services has been off the charts. Insurance rates may almost double for our employees, even with the discounted rates with Cityville, if we can get them again." Jennifer braces herself to notify her employees of the options. The business has done well this year, and she had hoped to give well-deserved raises. Now, she will either (a) need to put that money into covering the higher cost of the insurance premiums, reflecting higher utilization by the employees—meaning no raises again this year—or (b) switch to a different plan in which the employees need to contribute much more to their premium, which actually functions as a cut in overall take-home pay.

Floyd and Jennifer meet for coffee after work. "What a terrible day!" Jennifer laments, "I am going to need to give my employees the equivalent of a pay cut, one way or another, due to the increase in premiums." "What a wonderful day," Floyd beams, "I am going to be able to give my staff a raise due to the increased utilization of the hospital."

These scenarios, although simplistic, illustrate that one group's cash is another group's cost. In fee-for-service health care, there is a misalignment between (a) the hospital's business case to maximize consumption of services used by paying customers and (b) the economic case of other businesses, which instead have an incentive to hold down health care use, and thus cost, so that money is available for other aspects of their industry or for direct compensation to employees. The individual business case for the hospital is also at odds with the overall social case, in which the costs of products made in the United States compete with products in a global market, where non-U.S. labor and health care costs are much lower. So, what is good for American hospitals and other health providers in fee-for-service is not necessarily good for Americans in general. The equation is even more complicated, however, in that the drugs and equipment used in hospitals may be manufactured by U.S. companies that do gain financially when health care use increases. Recall, however, that nonprofit insurance companies are the middlemen between employers and health care, gathering the money from individuals and the organization to have it spread across individuals as needed. There is a great deal of rhetoric and occasional venom against insurance companies and, although there is a level of administrative costs associated with insurance companies, the rates also reflect the use of services by those in the insurance pool. On the surface, these may seem like economic issues. They are also ethical issues nurses can influence. Nurses, however, may get caught in situations in which they feel powerless to enact change or even to understand all the dynamics at play.

Simon is a 28-year-old with a history of substance abuse and ensuing pericarditis, resulting in mitral valve prolapse. He has a mitral valve replaced in August and following a 2-month hospitalization, was discharged on antibiotic therapy. Six months later, Simon returns, in need of a repeat surgery. Simon did not complete his antibiotic therapy as prescribed and has returned to his drug habit. The surgeon states that he will not do repeat surgery on Simon. Gloria, the RN, cannot decide what she thinks about this. Is the refusal to treat just? Is it unjust? Was Simon merely bearing the consequences of his actions and inactions, or did the health system have a moral obligation to treat Simon? Simon has insurance coverage through Medicaid, yet Gloria also understands that others bear the financial consequences of Simon's behaviors, as well as that of the surgeons, should Simon have expensive complications with— or without—surgery. Gloria wishes she had some system to help her think through the moral twists and turns so that she could come to a resolution and to feel that the right thing was done.

What is Gloria to do in this case? How can she discern which action is morally sound? We turn to these issues in the next section.

MORAL CONDUCT OF NURSES IN CONTEMPORARY COMPLEXITY

Nurses have a contract with society. In return for the privilege of being professionals, professionals must place the best interest of those they serve at the center of their actions and decisions. A police officer, for example, does not carry a gun and have a form of authority "just because." In their contract with society, police have special privileges in society in exchange for an obligation to "serve and protect." Similarly, nurses, physicians, and other health professionals have special privileges in society, including being privy to some of the most intimate and vulnerable times in an individual or family's life. In exchange, health professionals have the responsibility to serve the best interests of individual *and* societal health. Yet, what constitutes best interest can be difficult to discern. According to the Institute of Medicine (2013), roughly one third of what is done in health care does not make a difference at all. Fineberg (2012; also cited in Redberg, 2012) suggests that hundreds of billions to a whopping trillion dollars are spent on care that does not make a difference. Worse yet, sometimes health care actions harm rather than heal. Hospital-based preventable harm is estimated at epidemic proportions of over 400,000 patients/year (James, 2013), with other studies suggesting that adverse events occur in one third of hospitalizations (Classen et al., 2011). These findings suggest that some care not only creates economic harm, but also bodily and/or emotional injury. The *more is better* ethical goalpost is clearly misplaced, and new, more robust ethical models to guide health care are necessary.

Emerging Ethical Systems

Classic "universal principles" of health care, such as autonomy, beneficence, and nonmaleficence, have not incorporated patients' ethical obligations, nor have they easily held a creative synergistic balance between the individual and the population that discernibly serves both simultaneously. Similarly, classical ethical systems do not easily enable the clinician to incorporate population and financial considerations in their moral guideposts. In response, a new moral framework has been proffered by Faden and colleagues (2013). This framework is grounded in the Institute of Medicine call for a *health care learning system* in which the generation of new knowledge for the improvement of care is an explicit value. Such improvement includes cost, quality, and sustainability as foundational to fairness. These authors note, "Securing just health care requires a constantly updated body of evidence about the effectiveness and value of health care interventions and of alternative ways to deliver and finance health care" (p. S17). This inclusion of finance and testing of alternative delivery models as moral obligations offers additional reasons for nurses to be full participants in care redesign. It also underscores the importance of the evidence-based practice movement as an ethical obligation.

Health Care Learning System Ethical Framework Elements

The framework of Faden and colleagues (2013) delineates seven *fundamental obligations*—again, note that these are *moral obligations*—as follows:

1. The obligation to respect patients
2. The obligation to respect clinician judgment
3. The obligation to provide optimal care to each patient
4. The obligation to avoid imposing nonclinical risks and burdens
5. The obligation to address unjust inequalities
6. The obligation to conduct continuous learning activities that improve the quality of clinical care and health care systems
7. The obligation of patients to contribute to the common purpose of improving the quality and value of clinical care and the health care system

Unlike some other ethical schema, patient autonomy (embedded in item 1) does not trump all other considerations; all obligations must be held in concert. This framework demands accountability for a new set of systems from the nurse and also asks that patients participate in heretofore unprecedented ways. One example considers patient privacy issues in the era of big data. The policy tension revolves around controversy on whether or not patients should be able to opt out of having their personal data included in all-payer claims databases. These databases are ultimately used in cost containment and quality tracking and improvement. One argument would hold that the patient's right to autonomy and self-determination supports the idea that every patient has the right to refuse inclusion in the database. Conversely, Bates and colleagues (2014) reference Faden and colleagues and note that "patients have a moral obligation to contribute to the common purpose of improving the quality and value of clinical care" (p. 1129). The magnitude of this difference—the difference between a stance in which moral conduct consists in following patient wishes and one in which the patient has a moral obligation to the common good, the population as a whole—cannot be overstated. To this author's knowledge, An Ethics Framework for a Learning Health Care System (Faden et al., 2013) is the first definitively population-inclusive moral code offered for health and health care.

Ethics and the Role of the Nurse: Role Fidelity

Yet another universal principle of health care ethics is that of *role fidelity*. This principle means that professionals must be responsible and function within and to their role. An example might be an airline pilot. The pilot is responsible to the role of flying the plane safely. She must arrange her life and time to be faithful to the responsibilities of the role. Prior to the flight, she must rest appropriately and avoid any substances that might cloud her judgment. What if the pilot has hemorrhoids, is upset about a child or partner, or just plain grumpy? It does not matter. The pilot must fly the plane impeccably; many lives depend on it. Similarly, nurses have an ethical obligation to the role of nurse. So, what is the nurse's obligation in Simon's case? Conversely, what is Simon's obligation to the situation, given that his behavior likely was an antecedent to his condition? To what extent does it matter that his behavior may be related to or have an etiology of anything from poverty to adverse childhood events?

More information about Simon would be necessary to fully resolve the moral dilemma about his care. It is likely, however, that the present system is designed to fail Simon. Perhaps he did not have the social support to assure compliance with his postsurgical regime. Perhaps he is homeless, and recovering from surgery seemed less pressing than surviving the night. Perhaps he did not have transportation to obtain his medication, and the public transportation system was simply too daunting. Systems redesigned to ensure that Simon had the social support for the transition out of the hospital should be an essential nursing skill set, given nurses' knowledge of what is necessary in postacute care as well as nursing's community-inclusive education. Consistent with the model of Faden and colleagues (2013), nurse engagement with system redesign to assure that the system does not fail Simon and others is as essential to nurses' moral code as is patient confidentiality. Chapter 8 details several additional models that can support nurses' development as moral agents and offer additional perspectives on the complexity, promise, and perils of clinical decision making in an era of reform.

Thought Questions

1. What forms of care do you see that make a tangible, substantive, long-term difference? What forms of care do you see as futile?

2. What is the cost–benefit ratio of these? In other words, when you see care that makes a difference, what is given up for the cost of that care?

3. Have you seen patients harmed by care? What system, policy, or practice changes could have prevented that harm?

4. What does it mean for a nurse to be part of a learning health care system? What sort of learning and knowledge should he or she have? What sorts of contributions are essential?

5. Should patients be obligated to contribute to health care in the ways envisioned in the ethical model of Faden and colleagues? Justify your answer.

Exercise

1. Prepare a presentation for your peers that details the pros and cons of considering economics in the ethics of health care.

Quiz

TRUE OR FALSE

1. One limitation of traditional universal principles of health care ethics is that they have focused on the impact of clinical decision making on population health.

2. The term *beneficence* refers to the avoidance of doing harm.

3. Nurses are consistently rated as the most trusted professionals in the United States.

4. An Ethics Framework for a Learning Health Care System, offered by Faden and colleagues, is similar to traditional universal principles of health care ethics because both include a moral obligation for individual patients to contribute to the common purpose of improving the quality of care, the value of clinical care, and the health care system.

5. The term *role fidelity* refers to a professional's moral obligation to be faithful to the responsibilities of the role.

6. In general, socioeconomic status is associated with educational attainment.

7. Overtreatment and overutilization of health care may worsen population health disparities because the cost of these services erodes the social capacity to invest in other segments of the economy such as education and job creation.

8. In general, health care providers have had little accountability for the broader impacts of their clinical decision making on population health.

9. The term *nonmaleficence* refers to "doing good."

10. In fee-for-service reimbursement models, the hospital business case to maximize the amount of services used is at odds with the social needs for lower health care costs.

MULTIPLE CHOICE

11. Ethinomics
   A. Is a term coined by medical ethicist Merrill Mathews
   B. Refers to the convergence of economics and ethics in public policy
   C. Both A and B
   D. Neither A nor B

12. Classic universal principles of health care ethics include
   A. Autonomy
   B. Beneficence and nonmaleficence
   C. Both A and B
   D. Neither A nor B

13. Ethical tensions can exist when ethical principles suggest competing approaches: For example, a patient insists on a particular treatment that the provider feels will not benefit the patient, but instead cause harm. This example illustrates tensions between
   A. Justice and autonomy
   B. Autonomy and nonmaleficence
   C. Confidentiality and autonomy
   D. Confidentiality and justice

14. Hospital-based preventable harm
   A. Over the past decade has dramatically diminished in the U.S. health care system
   B. Has both cost and ethical dimensions
   C. Both A and B
   D. Neither A nor B

15. Intergenerational justice
    A. May be negatively impacted when one U.S. age cohort receives health care and other services at the expense of another
    B. May be negatively impacted when women receive health care and other services and men do not
    C. Both A and B
    D. Neither A nor B

REFERENCES

Adler, N., & Newman, K. (2002). Socioeconomic disparities in health: Pathways and policies. *Health Affairs, 21*(2), 60–76.

Bates, D., Saria, S., Ohno-Machado, L., Shah, A., & Escobar, G. (2014). Big data in health care: Using analytics to identify and manage high-risk and high cost health care. *Health Affairs, 33*(7), 1123–1131. doi:10.1377/hlthaff.2014.0041

CMS.gov. (2012). *National health expenditures data.* Retrieved February 24, 2015, from http://www.cms.gov/Research-Statistics-Data-and-Systems/Statistics-Trends-and-Reports/NationalHealthExpendData/NationalHealthAccountsHistorical.html

Classen, D., Resar, R., Griffin, F., Federico, F., Frankel, T., Kimmel, N., . . . James, B. (2011). "Global trigger tool" shows that adverse events in hospitals may be ten times greater than previously measured. *Health Affairs, 30*(4), 581–589.

Eddy, D. (1996). *Clinical decision making: From theory to practice.* Sudbury, MA: Jones & Bartlett.

Faden, R., Kass, N., Goodman, S., Pronovost, P., Tunis, S., & Beauchamp, T. (2013). An ethics framework for a learning health care system: A departure from traditional research ethics and clinical ethics. *Hastings Center Report, 42*(s1), S16–S27.

Fineberg, H. (2012). A successful and sustainable health system—How to get there from here. *New England Journal of Medicine, 366,* 1020–1027. doi:10:1056/NEJMsa1114777

Gallup Corporation. (2013). *Honesty/ethics in professions.* Retrieved January 22, 2014, from http://www.gallup.com/poll/1654/honesty-ethics-professions.aspx

Institute of Medicine. (2013). *Best care at lower cost: The path to continuously learning health care in America.* Washington, DC: National Academies Press.

James, J. (2013). A new, evidence-based estimate of patients harms associated with hospital care. *Journal of Patient Safety, 9*(3), 122–128. doi:10.1097/PTS.0b013e3182948a69

Mathews, M. (1999). *The role of economics and ethics in public policy debates. National Center for Policy Analysis.* Retrieved September 17, 2014, from http://www.ncpa.org/sub/dpd/index.php?Article_ID=11814

Newacheck, R., & Benjamin, A. (2004). Intergenerational equity and public spending. *Health Affairs, 23*(5), 142–146.

Redberg, R. (2012). *Less is more.* Retrieved from http://iom.edu/Global/Perspectives/2012/LessIsMore.aspx

Schaller, B. (2008). *Understanding bioethics and the law: The promise and perils of the brave new world of biotechnology.* Westport, CT: Greenwood.

ADDITIONAL MODELS TO GUIDE ETHICAL DECISION MAKING

FOLLOWING COMPLETION OF this chapter, you will be able to

- Compare and contrast utilitarianism, deontology, and virtue ethics
- Describe Rawls's theory of justice
- Discuss an ethic of caring
- Consider the impact of ethical decision making models on health care
- Discern moral distress

Chapter 7 detailed some of the complex interactions that can make it difficult to understand the full ethical dimensions of health care decision making in contemporary culture. The limitations and often conflicting nature of the very principles that are to guide ethical decision making were also illustrated. Chapter 8 builds on that knowledge to detail overarching models of ethical decision making that take yet a different approach. Three models are reviewed. These are

1. Consequence-based ethical decision making (utilitarianism)
2. Rule-based ethical decision making (deontology), with an emphasis on Rawls's theory of justice
3. Virtue-based ethics and an ethic of caring

CONSEQUENCE-BASED DECISION MAKING

Consequence-based decision making is grounded in the idea that decisions should be made so that the greatest good can happen for the greatest number of people. In the most extreme version of this model, the consequences—ends—justify the means, no matter how extreme. The American Nurses Association's *Code of Ethics for Nurses* (2001) offers an example of consequence-oriented decision making that is very familiar to nurses: triage in a disaster situation. Rather than place extensive resources to treat just one person, in crisis situations, triage deploys resources—both human and material—to maximize the number of people who survive, even at the expense of the few. A more dramatic, more controversial example is the dropping of the first atomic bombs in Hiroshima and Nagasaki, which effectively brought an end to World War II (WWII). The British Broadcasting Company estimates that between 60,000 and 80,000 died instantly, with the heat so intense that some simply vanished in the explosion, thus making an exact count difficult. Many more died of the long-term effects of radiation sickness, with the final death toll calculated at 135,000 (BBC, 2012). Other sources suggest that the total number of casualties was 135,000 at Hiroshima alone, with another 64,000 at Nagasaki; again, a precise number is difficult to determine because of the mass confusion after the bombing and the fires that consumed many bodies (Atomic Archive, n.d.). The overall death toll for WWII is suggested to be roughly 50 to 70 million people. The war ended within a week of the bombing. Did the perceived good, the end of the war, outweigh the deaths of innocent civilians? This example illustrates the painful trade-offs that bookend a consequence-oriented approach, as an attempt is made to maximize the good of the many, even when individuals are trampled on along the way.

Nurses and Consequence-Oriented Decision Making

Consequence-oriented decision making is also called *utilitarianism*. Nurses may use consequence-oriented decision making, often without being aware that there is an ethical dilemma, even though it may be on a microscale compared to the WWII example.

Ruth, RN, is working on a short-staffed night. She is concerned that Mr. Smith needs extra time and attention right now, but she has five other patients and knows that spending the time with Mr. Smith means

> *the others will not have as much of her time and attention. Walking past Mr. Smith's room, she hears him calling for her. She feels a pang of discomfort as she hurries to the next room, but feels it is the right thing to do, given the demands of the other patients.*

Limitations of consequence-orientated decision making include the impossibility of imagining and tracing forward all the consequences of actions and inactions. Moreover, if actions are to be directed toward consequences that increase "the good," how is the "good" defined, and by whom? Finally, if the focus is entirely on consequences, any act can conceivably be justified, no matter how harmful to the few. For many people, this focus does not meet a criterion of ethical decision making, no matter how many people are ultimately positively impacted.

DEONTOLOGY: RULE-BASED DECISION MAKING

In contrast, the orientation in rule-based decision making is that the ethical or moral stance is determined by adherence to a rule, principle, or duty. Rule-based ethical decision making is also called *deontological ethics* or *deontology*, from the Greek term for *duty*. In this moral schema, the ends cannot justify the means and, instead, an entirely different criterion is used, specifically the aforementioned rule. In the strictest conceptualization of such decision making, the rule must be followed, regardless of the consequences. If, for example, the rule is "thou shall not kill," there can be no taking of another's life, regardless of the consequence.

Rawls's Theory of Justice

John Rawls offers a fresh perspective on deontology in his highly influential texts *A Theory of Justice* (Rawls, 1999) and *Justice as Fairness* (Rawls, 2001). Rawls suggests, among other things, that in a just society, all individuals have the same claim on basic liberties. To achieve this, he suggests that social systems should be organized from the *original position*. This original position refers to a sort of thought experiment in which the basic organization of society is viewed from what Rawls termed a *veil of ignorance*, in which participants do not know their position, status, race, and gender. Thus, societal rules can be set up from a position of impartiality. How would, for example, health care be constructed if a participant did not know if he or she were a wealthy millionaire or a homeless veteran with posttraumatic stress disorder? Rawls argues that systems created referencing the original position with the veil of ignorance would have fair policies and procedures that protect the vulnerable and provide basic liberties to all.

VIRTUE ETHICS

Both consequence-oriented decision making and deontological decision making differ from *virtue ethics*. In virtue ethics, the emphasis is not on consequences or rules, but on character development such that the individual inherently functions from an ethical place as a morally developed person. Inspired by Aristotle, virtues such as courage and fortitude are viewed as inherent characteristics of humans, yet need nurturing. A challenge in virtue-based ethics is that it does not provide specific guidance on how to act in a particular situation. Nor are there clear directions, other than to act as a virtuous person acts.

An Ethic of Caring

Another variant of virtue-based ethics, *an ethic of caring*, is common in professional nursing and thus deserves particular note. In many ways, it is difficult for contemporary nurses to fully appreciate the radical departure from previous ways of thinking that Carol Gilligan's (1982) groundbreaking work offered. Aptly titled *In a Different Voice*, Gilligan challenged notions originally promulgated by Kohlberg (1958, 1984), whose description of six stages of moral development was based on samples that were exclusively male. Kohlberg's orientation conceived laws, rights, and justice as elements of the more evolved moral reasoning. When women were included in those studies, women's moral reasoning was often defined as less sophisticated and developed. Gilligan (1982) questioned the moral theory development that had been dominated by studies of men and offered an alternative perspective that demonstrated ethical decision making based on the values of caring and responsibility.

USING THESE MODELS IN CLINICAL DECISION MAKING

Nurses employ moral reasoning in *everyday ethics*. These commonplace ethical issues may not be as dramatic as end-of-life or human genome decision, but they are real and just as important or even more important because they are within the authority of the nurse to address directly. In the following scenario, Lou tries out different models to deal with an issue that is creating moral anxiety for her.

Lou is not sure what to do. She thinks that one of the providers in her practice, Dr. Sampson, is upcoding, using billing codes that are reimbursed at higher levels than what Lou sees as the correct code for the care. Lou ponders what to do and recalls her class on ethical decision making models. She likes Dr. Sampson and thinks that a moral reasoning involving caring would mean talking to Dr. Sampson. Unfortunately, this does not go well. Dr. Sampson says that the billing code is none of Lou's concern. Moreover, Dr. Sampson says that it is appropriate to be paid more. The consequence of not upcoding, argues Dr. Sampson, would mean that the practice would not have enough money to stay afloat and many of their staff would lose their positions. Now Lou is even more confused. Could it be okay to upcode? She recalls that in virtue-based ethics, a virtuous person should know exactly what to do. Lou does not know what to do, or even what the options are, so she does not find virtue ethics to be a helpful guide in this particular situation.

Lou recalls another model, consequence-oriented ethical decision making, but she is also conflicted about the consequences. Yes, there is the local impact on the practice, but what about the impact on the patients who are being billed at higher levels than they should be? One consequence is higher taxes and insurance premiums; in addition, patients with larger deductibles and copayments would be directly financially impacted. Lou now turns to rule-based ethical decision making. "What is the rule?" Lou wonders. Lou decides that more information might guide her. She searches the web and finds that upcoding is actually illegal and is considered a form of fraud! Lou now feels confident that she has something to help her through this situation. She checks the whistleblower protection in her health system and is pleased to find it intact and that it will support her taking action. Lou contacts the state Board of Nursing for assistance in navigating the reporting of this illegal practice.

In this scenario, the ethical issue quickly turned into a legal one as well, perhaps making a rule-based ethical approach a logical case. Legal dimensions, however, are not always the case in ethical dilemmas. Larson (2013), for example, suggests that the top ethical issue in health care is balancing care quality and efficiency. Yet in some cases, parameters that are designed to support high-quality outcomes instead create quality and ethical conflicts (Rambur, Vallett, Cohen, & Tarule, 2013). These authors detail metric-driven harm resulting from provider behavior that focuses the patient's care on achieving a metric rather than on taking the whole of the patient's preferences into consideration, a scenario that is incentivized when metrics are linked to payment of a physician or hospital. The 2014 Veterans Affairs scandal is a high-profile example. Rather than correctly reporting the inappropriately long wait times that veterans seeking service faced, a shadow set of publicly recorded reports manipulated the data to meet financially rewarding targets (Hicks, 2014). Metric-driven harm can, however, be even more subtle. Consider the example of Sam, RN.

Sam is confused. As a new team leader in the accountable care organization (ACO) of the Big Valley, he is excited about the intentional strategies to apply best practices and evidence-based practice to enhance quality of care and contain costs. As part of an ACO shared savings program, expenses less than projected are shared between the payer and the ACO, thus providing an incentive for efficient, appropriate care—provided certain quality metrics are met. As he reviews the quality metrics for shared savings, Sam is puzzled to see routine mammogram on the list of quality metrics. He had assumed that the metric triggers to achieve shared savings would be irrefutable. Yet, although not an uncommon screening practice, there is controversy on the value of routine mammograms, given mounting evidence that as the result of a mammogram, women are treated for something that would have never harmed them (Bleyer & Welch, 2012; Welch & Frankel, 2011). Sam understands that the quality metrics are intended to drive behavior and will! Sam knows that the need to report on this metric will cause more providers to order mammograms. On the surface, this may seem like an acceptable action, but his review of the literature causes Sam to question if routine mammogram is indeed a best practice or even evidence based. He also ponders the very large randomized control trial that found no difference in death rates among women who underwent screening and those who did not (Miller, Wall, Baines, Sun, To, & Narod, 2014). Sam uneasily wonders if this so-called quality measure may actually harm more than help. Sam is experiencing ethical tension.

Sam needs help to sort this out, so he contacts a mentor, the quality director at a large ACO in another state. Nurse Mentor states that their organization has just decided to "take the hit" on that metric and receive a negative score because they find the evidence against routine mammogram compelling and will not push routine screenings. Instead of incentives driving the behavior with an organizational goal of reaching a high level of routine screening among their client population, the decision is left to the patient and the provider, based on a more individual reference point. Sam brings this information to his leadership team, concerned about metric-driven overtreatment.

Sam's meeting with the senior team does not go well. The consensus of the group, without reviewing the literature, is that mammogram is a good thing, and a metric of ordering mammograms is a metric to be met. Sam also recalls that such imaging is a profitable business in his hospital. Sam is uncomfortable with this decision, which he feels has been made without real consideration. He feels both a sense of not knowing what to do, a moral dilemma between two somewhat unattractive alternatives, but also moral distress. Sam recalls the fundamental principle of nonmaleficence, but feels totally stuck on how to resolve this dilemma. (See Box 8.1 for a definition of moral distress.)

Box 8.1

What Is Moral Distress?

Austin (2007) suggests that *"moral distress* distinguishes moral dilemma—situations of not knowing how to act—from what is experienced when one believes one knows how to act but is thwarted by constraints. There is a sense of being morally responsible, but unable to change what is happening." (p. 84, emphasis in the original)

MORAL DISTRESS

The confluence of rapid change, limitations in nurses' authority span, and providers' education and socialization to maximize treatment has created a phenomenon notable among nurses termed *moral distress*. Moral distress differs from a *moral dilemma* in which the individual does not know what to do when caught between two or more equally dubious avenues. Instead, moral distress occurs when an individual feels morally confident about a certain action, but is unable to enact reconciling change due to power differentials or other organizational issues.

Contributing elements in producing moral distress include finances, power differences between disciplines, and conflicting goals and philosophy among health care providers (Corley, 2002; Sporrong, Hoglund, & Arnetz, 2006). It has also been suggested that moral tensions and strain can impel actions that modify the working environment and create moral well-being or *moral eustress* within a more *virtuous organization* (Rambur, Vallett, Cohen, & Tarule, 2010). In such a scenario, the nurse brings knowledge, skills, and experience to create organizational or systems change to better align the milieu with an informed moral compass and in so doing to also improve the organization.

ETHICS OF REFORM AND COST CONTAINMENT

The heretofore-described examples illustrate ethical issues at the intersection of clinical practice, organizational culture, and care market incentives. Other ethical issues are overarching. Saloner and Daniels (2011), for example, argue that the ethics of affordable health care coverage is rooted in "a societal obligation to protect fair *equality of opportunity*" (p. 816, emphasis added). This equality of opportunity has two major components. The first relates to the protection of health and normal functioning, so the individual has the basic opportunity to participate in society. The second aspect is financial protection, that is, ensuring that health care costs do not disproportionately erode opportunities for some, thus violating the ethical principle of fairness. Contrast, for example, the impact of an overall health care cost burden (premiums and out of pocket) of $10,000 for an individual who makes $30,000 per year with the impact of the same cost burden on someone making $200,000 per year. For the low-wage worker, the impact of the cost of health care is pronounced and erodes fair opportunity. These authors conclude that the Affordable Care Act is a corrective strategy in the right direction, but note that cost containment and alternative strategies that more equally distribute the cost burden, such as a more progressive tax structure, are necessary. By extension, care that is unnecessary creates cost without value and is therefore unethical. Thus, using Sam's dilemma as an example, everything we do or do not do matters.

Waste in the U.S. System

Unnecessary care and overtreatment are just one category of waste in the U.S. system. Berwick and Hackbarth (2012) identify the following forms of waste as representing 18% to 37% of health care spending: failures of care delivery, failures of care coordination, administrative complexity, pricing failures, and overtreatment. When fraud and abuse are added, including such things as the upcoding example, the cost to the U.S. health system is estimated to range from 21% to a whopping 47%, with a midpoint estimate of 34%—just over one third of U.S. health care spending (see Figure 8.1, adapted from Berwick and Hackbarth, 2012). Clearly, nurses' involvement in care coordination and focused attention to prevent overtreatment are essential elements of *role fidelity* in the current era. (See Box 8.2 to review a definition of role fidelity.)

Waste Estimate in U.S. Health Care Spending (2011)

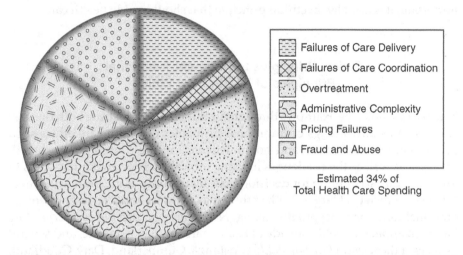

Failures of Care Delivery
Failures of Care Coordination
Overtreatment
Administrative Complexity
Pricing Failures
Fraud and Abuse

Estimated 34% of
Total Health Care Spending

Figure 8.1
Waste estimate in U.S. health care spending (2011).
Adapted from Berwick and Hackbarth (2012).

Box 8.2
What Is Role Fidelity?

Role fidelity is an ethical principle that requires a practitioner to practice faithfully within the professional role (Edge & Groves, 1999).

SUSTAINABILITY IS AN ETHICAL ISSUE

Another area of ethical challenge relates to the financial sustainability of the current health care system. The gross domestic product (GDP) is a measure of all goods and services produced by a nation. Health care expenditures have grown faster than the average annual growth of the GDP, and health care spending is projected to be nearly 20% of the total U.S. GDP by 2022 (CMS, n.d.). Imagine this in your own budget: 20 cents of every dollar going to health care, leaving only 80 cents for everything else. This, in turn, erodes opportunity for an array of choices that may have more personal value, particularly given the mixed outcomes of health care. The U.S. health care cost growth is unsustainable (Ginsburg et al., 2012), and it is thus logical to assume that what cannot be sustained will not be sustained. This raises questions about the impact of today's health care choices on future generations. Arguably, sustainability is not just important, it is actually an ethical principle that should guide health care.

Ethical Principles to Augment Traditional
Principles of Health Care Ethics

Taken as a whole, the examples throughout this chapter illustrate both the usefulness and shortcomings of traditional principles of health care ethics such as autonomy, beneficence, and nonmaleficence in the contemporary health care era, as well as the challenges in using ethical decision making models to guide action. Accounting for decision making not only at the individual level but also by society at large—both at the time of service and also over intergenerational time—is conceptually taxing. Nevertheless, such *full cost accounting* has been applied to fields outside of health care for over a decade, and several aspects of the *science of sustainability* (Costanza, Cumberland, Daly, Goodland, & Norgaard, 1997) offer parameters that translate to health care with ease. These include economic efficiency and distributional equity. The concept of distributional equity can be best understood by way of the obverse concept of distribution inequity: For example, the combined wealth of the world's richest 85 individuals is equal to that of the bottom 3.5 billion people or that of half the world's total population; almost half of the world's wealth goes to the richest 1% of the population, with the other half going to the remaining 99% of the world's population (Oxfam, 2014). A third element of the science of sustainability includes expanded accountability horizons. Translating this concept to health care, providers are not just responsible to the person in front of them, but also for the cost of the care and the impact on unseen others, with the responsibility to maintain human well-being—individual and collective—over intergenerational time. Population health perspectives in some payment reform models begin to nudge providers in this direction, as do organizational and policy changes toward a more just society. But how does an individual nurse begin to take action?

NURSES ON BOARDS AND IN POLITICS

One avenue for nurses to create such organizational change is through hospital and health care governance board membership. Indeed, the highly influential *The Future of Nursing* (2010) report by the Institute of Medicine calls for more nurses on boards, in order to better serve the public through more direct inclusion of nursing knowledge at the governance and/or policy level. Board membership alters power dynamics and can remove the differentials that often impede nurses' full participation in needed change. Previous chapters have reviewed essential knowledge for nurses' membership on boards, such as payment models as well as ethical frameworks and rationales for these efforts. Nevertheless, many nurses may be unfamiliar with the structure and functions of boards and, importantly, how to gain access to board positions. These topics are the focus of Chapters 9 and 10, followed by a review of the political process in Chapter 11.

Thought Questions

1. What tools can nurses use to assure that the care they are involved in is necessary?

2. Imagine a scenario in which you, the RN, perceive the patient to be receiving care of little value. What do you do? What ethical principles and decision making approaches can help guide your actions?

3. Have you experienced moral distress in a work setting? What elements of the environment contributed? What organizational, structural, or other changes could have alleviated your distress?

4. Imagine you are working in a setting that is chronically short-staffed, and you worry that patient safety is compromised. What ethical principles are in conflict? Now develop a strategy for addressing this situation, using the previously described ethical decision making models. Which ones are most useful?

Exercise

1. Develop a presentation for your peers that details why cost containment, managing waste and overtreatment, and health reform are issues of ethics. Use ethics terminology.

Quiz

TRUE OR FALSE

1. One common example of nurses using consequence-oriented ethical decision making is triage.

2. The American Nurses Association has published a *Code of Ethics for Nurses*.

3. Another term for consequence-oriented ethical decision making is deontology.

4. Moral eustress is another term for moral well-being following successful resolution of a situation of moral tension.

5. Gilligan's *ethic of caring* counters studies of moral reasoning that had been developed primarily using males as research subjects.

6. Rawls's approach to moral reasoning is defined as creating the greatest good for the greatest number of people.

7. Nurses use a variety of different ethical decision making models in clinical settings.

8. One challenge with consequence-oriented ethical decision making is that the individual may be harmed in an effort to maximize the good of the many.

9. The term deontology is derived from the Greek term for *duty*.

10. Virtue ethics focuses on consequences and rule-based decision making.

MULTIPLE CHOICE

11. Elements of Rawls's *Theory of Justice* include
    A. Decision making from the *original position* within a *veil of ignorance*
    B. An emphasis on classic Aristotelian values such as courage
    C. Both A and B
    D. Neither A nor B

12. Moral distress
    A. Is the same as a moral dilemma
    B. Can occur when an individual feels morally confident about the most appropriate route of action, but is thwarted from taking that action due to a power differential or organizational issues
    C. Both A and B
    D. Neither A nor B

13. The science of sustainability includes which of the following concepts?
    A. Distributional equity
    B. Expanded accountability horizons
    C. Both A and B
    D. Neither A nor B

14. Kohlberg's six stages of moral development suggest that the highest stages of moral development are rooted in
    A. Laws and rights
    B. Caring
    C. Both A and B
    D. Neither A nor B

15. Virtue ethics
    A. Provides clear guidelines on how to proceed in morally challenging situations
    B. Focuses on character development
    C. Both A and B
    D. Neither A nor B

REFERENCES

American Nurses Association. (2001). *Code of ethics for nurses with interpretative statements*. Washington, DC: Author.

Atomic Archive. (n.d.). *The atomic bombings of Hiroshima and Nagasaki*. Retrieved August 8, 2013, from http://www.atomicarchive.com/Docs/MED/med_chp10.shtml

Austin, W. (2007). The ethics of everyday practice: Healthcare environments as moral communities. *Advances in Nursing Science, 30*(1), 81–88.

BBC. (2012). Fact file: Hiroshima and Nagasaki. *WW2 People's War*. Retrieved August 8, 2013, from http://www.bbc.co.uk/history/ww2peopleswar/timeline/factfiles/nonflash/a6652262.shtml

Berwick, D., & Hackbarth, A. (2012). Eliminating waste in US health care. *Journal of the American Medical Association, 307*(14), 1513–1516.

Bleyer, A., & Welch, H. G. (2012). Effects of three decades of screening mammography on breast-cancer incidence. *New England Journal of Medicine, 367*, 1998–2005.

CMS. (n.d.). *National health expenditure projections 2012–2022*. Retrieved February 24, 2014, from http://www.cms.gov/Research-Statistics-Data-and-Systems/Statistics-Trends-and-Reports/NationalHealthExpendData/downloads/proj2012.pdf

Corley, M. (2002). Nurse moral distress: A proposed theory and research agenda. *Nursing Ethics, 9*(6), 636–650.

Costanza, C., Cumberland, J., Daly, H., Goodland, R., & Norgaard, R. (1997). *An introduction to ecological economics*. Boca Raton, FL: CRC Press.

Edge, R., & Groves, J. (1999). *Ethics of health care: A guide for clinical practice*. Boston, MA: Delmar.

Gilligan, C. (1982). *In a different voice: Psychological theory and women's development*. Cambridge, MA: Harvard University Press.

Ginsburg, P., Hughes, M., Adler, L., Burke, S., Hoagland, G., Jennings, C., & Lieberman, S. (2012). *What is driving U.S. health care spending: America's unsustainable health care cost growth*. Princeton, NJ: Robert Wood Johnson Foundation, Bipartisan Policy Center.

Hicks, J. (2014). This memo shows that the VA knew of record manipulation in 2010. *Washington Post*. Retrieved September 24, 2014, from http://www.washingtonpost.com/blogs/federal-eye/wp/2014/05/20/this-memo-shows-that-the-va-knew-of-records-manipulation-in-2010/

Institute of Medicine. (2010). *The future of nursing: Leading change, advancing health*. Washington, DC: National Academies Press.

Kohlberg, L. (1958). *The development of models of thinking and choices in years 10 to 16* (PhD dissertation). University of Chicago, Chicago, IL.

Kohlberg, L. (1984). *The psychology of moral development: The nature and validity of moral stages—essays on moral development (Vol. 2)*. San Francisco, CA: Harper and Row.

Larson, J. (2013). Five top ethical issues in health care. *AMN Healthcare News*. Retrieved September 24, 2014, from www.amnhealthcare.com/latest-healthcare-news/five-top-ethical-issues-healthcare

Miller, A., Wall, C., Baines, C., Sun, P., To, T., & Narod, S. (2014). Twenty-five year follow-up for breast cancer incidence and mortality of the Canadian National Breast Screening Study: Randomised screening trial. *British Medical Journal, 348*, g366. doi:http://dx.doi.org/10.1136/bmj.g366

Oxfam. (2014). Working for the few: Political capture and economic inequality. *Oxfam Briefing Paper, 178*. Retrieved September 24, 2014, from http://www.oxfam.org/files/file_attachments/bp-working-for-few-political-capture-economic-inequality-200114-en_3.pdf

Rambur, B., Vallett, C., Cohen, J., & Tarule, J. (2010). The moral cascade: Distress, eustress, and the virtuous. *Journal of Organizational Moral Psychology, 1*(1), 41–54.

Rambur, B., Vallett, C., Cohen, J., & Tarule, J. (2013). Metric-driven harm: An exploration of unintended consequences of performance measurement. *Applied Nursing Research, 26*(4), 269–275.

Rawls, J. (1999). *A theory of justice*. Cambridge, MA: Harvard University Press

Rawls, J. (2001). *Justice as fairness: A restatement*. E. Kelly (Ed.). Cambridge, MA: Belknap Press.

Saloner, B., & Daniels, N. (2011). The ethics of the affordability of health insurance. *Journal of Health Politics, Policy and Law, 36*(5), 816–827. doi:10.1215/03616878-1407631

Sporrong, S., Hoglund, A., & Arnetz, B. (2006). Measuring moral distress in pharmacy and clinical practice. *Nursing Ethics, 13*(4), 416–427.

Welch, H. G., & Frankel, B. (2011). Likelihood that a woman with screen-detected breast cancer has had her "life saved" by that screening. *Archives of Internal Medicine, 17*(22), 2043–2046.

PULLING IT ALL TOGETHER: USING YOUR KNOWLEDGE OF HEALTH FINANCE, ECONOMICS, AND ETHICS TO INFLUENCE HEALTH AND HEALTH CARE

We have traveled through complex terrain together as we have navigated the twists, turns, and history of health care financing and reimbursement; plunged into deep waters of health care economics and what it means to nurses and to patients; and explored uses and limits of ethical theories to support moral reasoning and decision making. You now have the knowledge to be an influential force in health care, in your practice, but also in the world, more broadly. Nursing knowledge is necessary to shape health and health care beyond the borders of the bedside. But to do so, there are some additional pieces of information that are necessary.

First, how institutions are organized and governed is essential for influencing change as well as maintaining things that are working well. Imagine trying to help a cardiac patient if you did not know how the heart worked. Chapter 9 discusses organizations and their governance. As noted in the preface to this text, the Institute of Medicine (2010) made important health care recommendations in *The Future of Nursing: Leading Change, Advancing Health,* including a plea for more nurses to serve on governing boards. You might wonder if this is to serve nursing. Not at all! It is to serve patients and society by bringing what nurses know to the highest level of decision making and influence. Nevertheless, many nurses do not consider such roles for themselves or aspire to them. Do you? If not, Chapters 9 and 10 are dedicated to changing this. The goal is that you will consider such roles for yourself and mentor others to aspire and achieve, as well.

To accomplish this goal, Chapter 9 describes organizational types and differentiates between governance and management responsibilities. Because some of the readers of this text are undergraduate students seeking their first RN license, while others are more seasoned RNs seeking a baccalaureate or even a graduate degree, Chapter 9 laces in scenarios that describe organizational types from the perspective of a job seeker, in the hopes that the illustration will be useful to both the novice seeking a job and the seasoned professional exploring the pathways to the boardroom.

Chapter 10 describes the different routes to a board seat, reflecting different types of boards. It includes foundational information on how to run or participate in a meeting as well as a primer on financial terms you will hear in board meetings. Money is the language of power in the boardroom, so learn to speak it with authority.

But wait! Why stop with just board membership? Why not consider policy and politics? Chapter 11 provides information on ways to use all you have learned to be effectively involved in politics and influence health and health care policy.

Chapter 12 concludes with some closing reflections and thoughts for your future direction and ongoing self-development in the areas of finance, economics, and politics. So, let us start by sorting out some key basics on organizations.

GOVERNANCE AND ORGANIZATIONAL TYPE

FOLLOWING COMPLETION OF this chapter, you will be able to

- Describe the role, responsibilities, and differences among categories of oversight boards
- Detail the differences between governance and management
- Illustrate common management structures
- Describe the impact of the Sarbanes–Oxley Act on health care organizations

Jennifer enjoys her work as a neonatal intensive care nurse. Nevertheless, she sometimes wonders if there might be an easier way to make a living. As she leaves the unit, she notices the CEO giving a tour to a group of individuals dressed in expensive suits. "Boy, that would be the life," she muses, "high salary and just walk around all day." She wonders how people access these positions.

Now that you know the broader dimensions of health care, you are ready to enact change and influence policy. Yet to do so, an understanding of organizational structure is necessary; influence cannot be leveraged without knowing what levers to push, who is responsible for what, and the manner in which an organization is "wired together." Let us start with the chief executive officer (CEO) and the governing board to which the CEO reports.

To a harried staff nurse or student, it may seem that the CEO stands far above the fray and has enormous unilateral power. Although it is true that the CEO has broad responsibilities, the CEO, too, has a boss. This "boss" is the board of trustees (BOT).

ROLE OF THE BOARD OF TRUSTEES

The role of the BOT is to assure that the mission of the organization is met. A board member is expected to act in the best interest of the organization, with skill and due diligence. Indeed, board members may be sued for reckless or negligent behavior that harms an organization, a concept analogous to medical negligence or malpractice (see Box 9.1 for a description of *directors and operators liability insurance*, which provides protection to the board member in a manner analogous to medical malpractice insurance). Thus, when a wise nurse is a member of a governing board, he or she is thoughtful about board responsibilities and committed to giving the time and attention needed to be a diligent board member. At the same time, the reality of the responsibility should not be a deterrent to seeking board membership. No one board member has all the oversight skills necessary, which is why highly functioning boards are composed of individuals with diverse skills and perspectives.

Box 9.1
Directors and Operators Liability Insurance

An individual accepting a high-level board position is well advised to ascertain if he or she is covered by "directors and operators liability insurance" (D and O insurance)—insurance that provides financial protection to a board member in the event that he or she is sued in relation to actions or inactions as a board member. In a small organization with a relatively small budget and few financial assets, it may not be necessary to have D and O insurance; at the same time, that leaves board members potentially liable. Generally, D and O insurance is not necessary when serving on an advisory board, which by its very nature does not have fiduciary responsibility for the organization. Similarly, membership on a state or federal board is again a bit different because

---

actions are on behalf of that governmental entity, and thus there is protection for the board member through that entity. Contrast this, for example, with a hospital board in which a single board decision may mean multimillion- or even billion-dollar expenditures. Or, for example, failure to properly oversee a rogue chief executive officer (CEO) who causes harm to the institution could leave the board members liable for oversight failure. In these cases, D and O insurance would provide a form of insurance protection for financial liability, conceptually similar to medical malpractice insurance. Notably, the organization typically provides D and O insurance to board members, a likely essential approach in nonprofit boards where board members are not compensated for their time as board members.

Governance, Not Management

The board also hires the CEO, sets the CEO compensation package, reviews CEO performance, and—when necessary—removes the CEO. The board responsibility is *governance* rather than *management*. Thus, beyond this oversight of the CEO, management is not within the purview of the BOT. Healthy organizations strike a balance whereby the board is neither overinvolved in management details that are the rightful responsibility of the management team nor merely rubber stamping governance activities for which they are responsible. Succession planning—planning to assure continuity of leadership—is also an important but often overlooked responsibility of the board (Naylor, Behan, & Naylor, 2006). One way this is accomplished is by building "bench strength" among the senior leadership team. However, management of the senior leadership team is a management issue, rather than a governance issue, illustrating one challenge to the succession planning responsibility of the board.

Impact of Organizational Type

Because the work of the board is to ensure that the mission of the organization is met, organizations with different missions have different board orientations. Although this is important to understand when seeking to gain influence through board membership, organizational type impacts all elements of the work of the institution. Therefore, it is valuable to consider organizational mission and type—whether seeking or accepting a board position or even when seeking employment or considering a new job—to ensure that there is a fit between individual aspirations and values and the organization.

TYPES OF HOSPITALS AND HEALTH SYSTEMS

To better understand different organizational types—a skill essential for effective board membership—it may be illustrative to first consider organizational types with a more familiar scenario, that of a new graduate seeking the first RN position.

*Conner is considering his first RN position after graduating with his BS in Nursing from Prestigious University. He is interested in either moving to ski country or sun country and applies to positions throughout the western United States. He receives callbacks from several institutions and narrows it down to five. In trying to make a decision, he notes that all five institutions are very different from each other. One is a large **for-profit** institution; three are **nonprofit,** with one being associated with a university **academic medical center**, the second a nonprofit **community hospital**, and the third nonprofit, a **critical access hospital (CAH)**. The fifth institution falls into a still different category. It is an urban, inner-city **public hospital**. Conner knows he does not have the funds or emotional energy to interview at all five and needs to narrow down his job search. Perplexed, he calls his former mentor, Dr. Whitney. Dr. Whitney suggests that any of these institutions could be a great choice. "It is all a matter of fit," says Dr. Whitney. "Which mission seems like the best fit for your interests?" Conner realizes he has no real idea what Dr. Whitney is talking about, so he thanks him and decides to do a bit more homework on organizational types and missions.*

Although health care is delivered by different types of organization in the United States, as Conner's job search revealed, they fall into three broad categories: nonprofit, for-profit, and public. Nonprofit institutions are the most common in health care and human services, with Horwitz (2005) finding that two-thirds of hospitals are nonprofit, with the remainder split between for profit and public. For-profit hospitals are sometimes termed *investor owned*. Public institutions are financed through taxes. Also categorized as *governmental*, these may be state, county, city–county, city, hospital district, or federal entities (CBO, 2006).

Nonprofit and For-Profit Institutions

Let us consider the differing missions of nonprofit and for-profit institutions and how this impacts the board orientation. In each case, the BOT is responsible for assuring that the mission of the organization is met, yet there is a substantial distinction between missions of nonprofit and for-profit organizations. In for-profit organizations, the mission includes an explicit intention to return profits to owners or shareholders. Nonprofit organizations do not have owners or shareholders expecting dividends on their investments. Instead, financially healthy nonprofit organizations achieve a different sort of "profit" each year, in the form of a *budget surplus*. A budget surplus, sometimes called an *operating margin*, is intended to be garnered for an investment in the organization rather than being delivered or "paid" to owners or shareholders. A negative operating margin, a rather paradoxical term, means that a nonprofit organization spent more money than it received that year, an unsustainable situation for any organization. Thus, both these organizational types must bring in more money than they spend, with the difference being the intended use of those funds. These differing orientations create differences in organizational behavior, functioning, and even legal requirements. As one such example, nonprofit hospitals must demonstrate *community benefit* to retain nonprofit status for tax purposes. See Table 9.1 for additional differences between for profit and nonprofit hospitals.

Another lens through which to understand organizations is to discern if they are private or public. For example, private hospitals can be nonprofit

Table 9.1

Differences Between For-Profit and Not-for-Profit Hospitals

For Profit	Nonprofit
Not tax exempt—pays state and local property taxes	Does not pay state or local taxes
No community benefit requirement*	Must demonstrate community benefits in accordance with state and federal guidelines*
Owned by private investors or owned publicly by shareholders	Not owned
In general, provides care to a greater proportion of Medicaid-covered patients*	In general, provides more uncompensated care*

Source: *CBO (2006).

or for-profit organizations, but they both differ from public institutions, such as public hospitals that are funded through taxes. Service to indigent populations was the primary impetus for the growth of public hospitals, serving as a safety net for those who might not otherwise be able to access care. Such organizations may also have added services that address social determinants of health (Anderson, Boumbulian, & Pickens, 2004). Hence, governance of a hospital whose mission is to serve indigent or underserved populations would have very different goals and values than, for example, a private, for-profit hospital intent on returning profits to shareholders. It should also be noted that the role of public hospitals, traditionally offering safety net services to the uninsured and indigent, is uncertain in an era of universal financial access to health care (i.e., post–Affordable Care Act; California Healthline, 2010).

Mission, Hospital Type, and Reimbursement

Some hospital categories reflect unique missions and also have different reimbursement schedules. Using Conner's job search scenario as an example, there is a range of hospital types along a continuum from very small, rural hospitals that serve as *critical access*; to *community hospitals* that serve the more common and routine health care needs of their local community; to large, *tertiary* or even *quaternary* care centers that are referral centers for a region or even a nation, serving with very complex, highly unusual, specialized care. Tertiary and quaternary care centers may be affiliated with an *academic medical center*, which is a university-based teaching and research-oriented college of medicine, and possibly other health professional colleges. As with the public versus private hospitals, each of these different institutions would have very different missions and thus differing responsibilities for the governing body. For example, the mission of a tertiary care hospital with an academic medical center would include not only health care of the most critically and complexly ill, but also teaching health professionals and stewarding research. Quaternary care would be even more specialized, focused on management of highly uncommon conditions and experimental treatments. Contrast this with, for example, a CAH, which—by the Centers for Medicare and Medicaid (CMM) definition—must be in a rural area without other services nearby, furnish 24-hour emergency care 7 days a week, have no more than 25 inpatient beds, and have an average length of stay of 96 hours or less. Thus, a CAH exists to provide emergency services in remote areas, stabilization services in preparation for transfer to a tertiary care center, or short-term stays for relatively uncomplicated care. Importantly, CAHs are reimbursed at 101% of reasonable cost, as many would not be financially viable in the "marketplace" without this preferential reimbursement. Thus, the

---

Box 9.2

What Does It Mean to Hold Fiduciary Responsibility?

"Fiduciary duty is a legal duty to act solely in another party's interest. Parties owing this duty are called fiduciaries. The individuals whom they owe a duty are called principals. Fiduciaries may not profit from their relationship with their principals unless they have the principals' express informed consent. They also have a duty to avoid any conflict of interest between themselves or their principals or between their principals and the fiduciaries' other clients. *A fiduciary duty is the strictest duty of care recognized by the U.S. legal system.*"

Source: Legal Information Institute (n.d., emphasis added)

---

trustees must understand, or quickly become familiar with, the mission and funding streams of the institution for which they are responsible to execute their fiduciary responsibility (see Box 9.2). Again, understanding these differences in mission and scope is also useful for the novice in a job search.

Conner spent a great deal of time looking at the websites of the five institutions. He finds himself attracted to two very different institutions, the inner-city public hospital and the rural CAH. He realizes there is a commonality between these that he had not originally noticed. Both serve vulnerable, underserved populations, and he is drawn to this work. Conner decides to interview at only these two institutions. Excitedly, he tells his best friend, Jennifer, who is also a new graduate in a job search. "I don't understand you at all," says Jennifer. "Don't you want to be at the academic medical center, taking part in research? It would also be so easy to pick up your master's degree because of the affiliation with a university, or maybe even a DNP or PhD."

Conner shares that he is very confident that, despite their differences, the inner-city public hospital or the rural hospital are the best fit for him, and he will narrow it down further after the onsite visit. He is confident he can obtain his MS in other ways, maybe even via online courses. Jennifer decides instead to apply to the institutions that attract her: the tertiary care–academic medical center–university-affiliated hospital and one of the community hospitals. The community hospital is in a trendy

> *suburb that Jennifer likes, and she is not sure if the degree of specialization that RNs often have at a tertiary care hospital is the best fit for her, or if a slightly more general practice in a smaller, slightly less intense setting is a better match. She is confident, however, that one of the two is the best fit for her. Both Conner and Jennifer are pleased they have chosen nursing—there are so many organizational options.*

Note that as job seekers, Conner and Jennifer have choices as to which hospital type they are interested in and can determine which one feels like the best fit. This is typically not the case for nurses seeking board membership. As nurses access board positions (as discussed in Chapter 10), the process typically is facilitated through proximity, connections, and knowledge base relative to the organization's needs, so knowledge of all organizational types is helpful for a nurse seeking a board position. Finally, this example illustrated hospitals, which is among the most diverse category of organizational type. Home health agencies tend to be either for-profit or nonprofit and operate under a similar board structure. Other organizations, like accountable care organizations, are in evolution, but may be affiliated with several of these organizational types.

NAVIGATING GOVERNANCE– MANAGEMENT BOUNDARIES

> *Bethany is fuming! Newly elected as the president of the hospital nurses' union, she cannot understand why the board is so unresponsive to the union's demands. They have negotiated in good faith with the administrative bargaining team led by the vice president (VP) of human relations, but—in frustration—Bethany presented a passionate plea at the open session of the board of trustee meetings at both of the last two sessions. Both times the board listened politely, but nothing seemed to come of it. "Why doesn't the board do something?" she laments.*
>
> *Clara is dismayed. As the newly elected chair of the board of trustees, she hopes to foster a climate of inclusion and respect. Yet, the union's spectacles at the board's meetings are accelerating. Clara admires the fiery Bethany, sees much of her own young self in Bethany, and appreciates*

her zeal and passion for the work of the institution they both so clearly love. "But why does Bethany continue to bring management issues to the board?" wonders Clara. "Does she understand that union negotiations are management issues, and not under the purview of governance?" She considers telling Bethany directly, yet is concerned that Bethany would misperceive the intention. She decides that if the union contract is still unsettled next month and Bethany and her troops present again to the board, then she, Clara, will again politely thank her, but directly ask if she and the other union leaders understand that union negotiations are a management issue, not a governance issue, and thus not within the board's scope of responsibility and authority.

Perhaps one of the areas of greatest blurring for the nurse new to board work is to understand the difference between management and governance. Yet to appropriately apply influence, it is fundamental to understand the governance role of boards and differentiate it from management. With the exception of the CEO, who reports to the BOT, all senior management, sometimes called the *senior leadership team*, reports to the CEO, not the board.

The Senior Leadership Team

Different organizations divide the responsibility of senior management differently; however, a very common structure is the CEO—who may also hold the title of president—in the lead yet reporting to the board, with a chief financial officer (alternately titled VP for finance) and chief operating officer (COO—alternate titles include VP for operations) reporting to the CEO. In some organizations, the COO and chief nursing officer (CNO) are combined, with a title reflective of that role, such as VP for patient services. In other organizations, the CNO reports to the COO, while in still other settings, the reporting line is to the CEO or chief medical officer (CMO). CMOs typically report to the CEO. See Figure 9.1 for examples of different senior-level management structures commonly found within health care.

Why Do Reporting Lines Matter?

Reporting lines are important, as the further the line is from the CEO, the less likely the individual is to interact with and influence the CEO on a daily

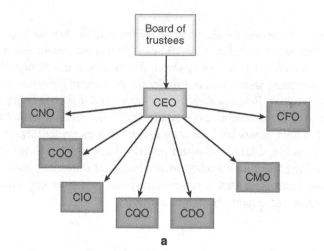

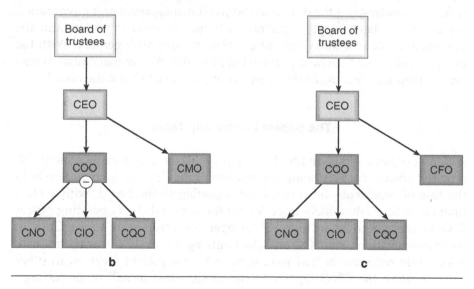

Figures 9.1a—c
Examples of different organizational senior leadership reporting lines.

CEO, Chief Executive Officer/President; COO, Chief Operating Officer/Vice President of Operations; CFO, Chief Financial Officer/Vice President of Finance; CIO, Chief Information Officer/Vice President of Information Management; CQO, Chief Quality Officer/Vice President of Quality; CMO, Chief Medical Officer/Vice President of Medical Affairs; CNO, Chief Nursing Officer/Vice President of Nursing basis, and the less likely they are to have board contact. An organization in which the CNO and CMO have similar authority and an equally broad *span of control* creates a very different sort of organization from one in which the CNO reports to the CMO, as just one example. The term span of control means the number of services, people, or functions for which an individual is responsible. Inherent in the definition is the notion that the individual has both the *responsibility* and the corresponding *authority* to execute that responsibility. Take a moment to review the organizational structure of some of the hospitals and agencies you have practiced in. Where is the most senior nurse leader located in the organizational structure?

Senior Leadership Positions Reflect Health Care Change: Who Is on the Team in Your Organization?

In the 21st century, two new, high-level roles have emerged: chief quality officer (CQO) and chief information officer (CIO). These may be stand-alone roles reporting to the president/CEO or—with a different title, reporting line, and level of influence—reporting only indirectly to the CEO/president, with the direct report being through a VP. Health care is also highly regulated and accountable to the public. Moreover, given that roughly 50% of health care is publicly funded through taxes, state and federal relations are an important interface for any contemporary organization. Thus, VPs for government relations and community relations are also common and typically report directly to the president/CEO. Depending on the size of the organization, this may be a conjoined position or two different posts occupied by two different individuals. Although less common in health care, higher education institutions—colleges and universities, for example—often have a chief diversity officer/VP for multicultural affairs among their senior leadership team. Understanding the roles and responsibilities of these individuals is very important for any nurse wanting to be influential in the corollary areas.

What About Fund-Raising?

The goal of raising external funds through philanthropy is an extraordinarily important realm in today's health care milieu. This arm of an institution is commonly structured in one of two ways. There may be a separate foundation with a separate board that is responsible for fund-raising or, instead, there may be a VP for development who reports to the CEO/president. In this latter configuration, the role may also include community outreach and public relationships, as well as marketing and press relation functions. This sort of position is often termed VP of advancement. Finally, the position of VP for innovation or VP for strategy and innovation is an emerging role, as institutions seek, and often struggle, to redefine themselves in a rapidly changing, resource-limited health care environment.

What Does It Mean to Be an Ex Officio Board Member?

In for-profit organizations, the CEO is sometimes also chair of the board. The CEO is typically an *ex officio* board member. Ex officio members are board members by virtue of being in a particular job role, and depending on the organization, ex officio members may be voting or nonvoting as prescribed in organizational bylaws. In academic medical centers, the dean of medicine is routinely an ex officio board member, yet inclusion of the dean of nursing in board membership is less common. This, in turn, creates a very different span of influence for the educational and research opportunities for the students represented by the dean. Moreover, aside from these potential ex officio board posts, nurses are markedly underrepresented on boards of health organizations. Myers (2008) notes that in a study of community health system governance, only 2.4% of board seats were held by nurses, in stark contrast to physicians, who held 22% of board seats.

THE RELATIONSHIP BETWEEN ORGANIZATIONAL STRUCTURE AND ORGANIZATIONAL VALUES

Why is the structure and makeup of this senior leadership team so important? Organizational structure reflects organizational values. It is illustrative to examine where in the hierarchy the most senior nurse is situated. To whom does the chief nurse report? This has implications not only for influence but also for span of control. A CNO who is also the COO and reports to the president/CEO has a very different span of control than one who, for example, reports through a COO or CMO.

The role of all of these individuals is senior management. The various VPs or "chiefs" report to the CEO/president, who in turn reports to the board. Sullivan (2013) elegantly describes the problems that can arise when new nurse leaders do not understand the senior management lines—for example, a new CNO preparing her first budget but going to the board chair for help, rather than to her immediate supervisor, the CEO. In the scenario detailed, the board chair—appropriately—chastises her. First, budget preparation is a management issue, and boards later approve the overall budget.

In other words, the board has fiduciary responsibility that includes budget approval as a form of governance oversight over the work of the management team that prepared the budget. Second, the new CNO could be perceived as insubordinate and attempting to circumvent her supervisor. In any case, no matter where he or she is positioned in an organization, the savvy nurse understands the reporting lines and roles.

THE ROLE OF BOARD COMMITTEES

Boards commonly divide their governance oversight into different working committees, termed *standing committees*. Although each board member has a legal, fiduciary responsibility to the overall mission of the organization, committees allow members with different expertise to bring those skills to board work in a more focused way. These various committees typically have a lead staff member from among the VPs—for example, the CQO would be a logical lead staff for the quality committee of the board. Common standing committees in health care organizations are listed in Box 9.3. Note, however, that the exact committee name would vary by organization. Typically, all work of the standing committees goes to the full board for approval. So, for example, the executive compensation committee will do foundational work to develop the CEO's compensation package, but implementation would require approval of the full board.

Box 9.3

Common Standing Board Committees

Audit committee

Finance committee

Quality committee

Development committee (unless there is a separate foundation responsible for fund-raising)

Facilities and planning committee

Nominating committee (generating names of qualified individuals for board membership)

Mission and ethics committee

Executive compensation committee (designs and reviews chief operating officer's [CEO's] compensation package)

Executive committee (usually consisting of all committee chairs, it is a powerful committee that often meets between board meetings to conduct business)

Committee Charters, Bylaws, and Ad Hoc Committees

Board committees typically have *charters* that delineate the role and responsibility of the committee. The rules for modifying the charter of a committee can be found in the *organizational* or *board bylaws*. Although organizational bylaws may seem arcane and cumbersome to read, bylaws codify organizational rules and are therefore an important item for thoughtful review by any new board member. Finally, boards may also form *ad hoc committees* and *advisory committees*. An ad hoc committee is a short-term, temporary committee that is formed to study and address a particular issue, report back to the full board, and then dissolve, whereas an advisory committee invites nonboard members with complementary areas of expertise to provide advice on key areas. A home health agency, for example, may have an end-of-life advisory board composed of palliative care experts, ethicists, social workers, and religious advisors/clergy. Such advisory boards do not have fiduciary responsibility (see Box 9.2) for the organization and offer advice without authority for governance or oversight of the CEO or president. They are a valuable way for an organization to connect community leaders and interested parties, ensuring that stakeholders and potential benefactors remain engaged in the work of the organization.

Governance boards have additional responsibility since the passage of the Sarbanes–Oxley Act of 2002, which is outlined in the next section.

THE SARBANES–OXLEY ACT

"How could it have happened?" Fred and Regina lost all the investments that they had carefully made over the course of a lifetime. A retired, former employee of Enron, Fred had felt well prepared for retirement. Now, 2 years into retirement, Enron's swift collapse—from an organization ranked as the world's seventh largest energy company in April 2001 to bankruptcy filing in December 2001—has wiped out all but Social Security payments for Fred and Regina. "You know what sticks most in my craw?" Fred asks Regina. "That as the stock value was falling, we couldn't sell our stocks but the brass—all the bosses—could. Someone needs to be sure this never happens to anyone else again."[1]

That "someone" was Congress, with the passage of the Sarbanes–Oxley Act of 2002.

Traditionally, the central role of a governing board has been to "act as a watch dog" (Nadler, Behan, & Nadler, 2006, p. 6) and to oversee the overall functioning of the organization as well as the CEO. A series of corporate scandals—Enron, as just one example—rocked the United States and resulted in passage of the Sarbanes–Oxley legislation, sometimes called SOX, in 2002. This legislation was designed to minimize the opportunity for fraud, financial mismanagement, and conflicts of interests among corporations and their leaders. Although SOX is directed to for-profit organizations, there has been substantial spillover to nonprofit organizations, including hospitals and health care organizations. Although only two provisions of SOX pertain directly to nonprofit organizations—whistleblower protection and stipulations related to document destruction—many nonprofit organizations have voluntarily adopted SOX provisions (Worth, 2013). Many of these adoptions seem inherently logical and ethical, such as the provision that prohibits organizational loans to board members or executives. A more complex and nuanced SOX provision relates to audit committee responsibilities.

The Board Audit Committee

Prior to SOX, the typical role of the audit committee detailed in most audit committee charters was responsibility for selection of external auditors, recommendations for payment of external auditors, review of the performance of external auditors, and assessment of the accounting report. The SOX act dramatically changes the role and responsibility of audit committees, requiring more independent conversations between the audit committee of the board and the independent auditor, exclusive of an intermediary function by the CEO and senior leadership. Logically, it makes sense for the board, which has a fiduciary responsibility to the organization and for CEO performance, to have the opportunity for assessment of financial operations of the organization independent of the CEO and senior management involvement. Yet, as Rossiter (2004) notes, this requirement constitutes a substantial change in the manner in which business had been conducted, given that this board committee–auditor communication is "without management functioning as a filter or even providing context" (p. 2). Rossiter further notes that the audit committee may be required to make many more difficult judgments than in the pre-SOX era, potentially diminishing the pool of those willing, or prepared, to serve on the audit committee. Finally, each member of the committee must be an audit expert or explain why such expertise is not necessary. In health care organizations, midsized and large hospitals typically have a similar overall audit committee orientation, with the audit committee having direct interaction with auditors and at least one member of the committee holding a firm background in finance (Bader, 2010).

The Board Quality Committee

Some authors also suggest that a greater understanding of quality of care on the part of board members is essential. Bader (2010) proposes that there should be "quality audits," a concept conceptually analogous to financial audits. Warden (cited in Myers, 2008) highlights the important contribution nurses bring to boards in this area, stating:

> The nurse brings the ability to translate and demonstrate evidence-based kinds of safety and quality improvements to the board and brings an in-depth understanding of the patient care process. The nurse can make or break an institution in terms of quality and safety. (p. 12)

Thus, nurses are well positioned to play pivotal roles on boards, provided they can access board membership. This latter issue, accessing board membership, is the focus of the next chapter.

Thought Questions

1. A colleague reports frustration at the number of vice presidents in her organization. What thoughts can you share about the roles of these vice presidents?

2. What organizational structure do you see as most optimal for nursing practice and why?

3. Define the following key terms:

   Academic medical center   Advisory board or
                                committee
   Ad hoc committees

Budget surplus

Charter

Community benefit

Community hospital

Critical access hospital

Directors and operators insurance

Ex officio committee member

For-profit organization

Fiduciary responsibility

Governance

Investor-owned institution

Management

Nonprofit organization

Operating margin

Organizational bylaws

Public hospital

Quaternary care center

Senior leadership team

Span of control

Standing committee

Tertiary care center

Exercise

1. Develop a presentation to share with your peers that describes the various types of hospitals in the United States. What are the strengths and limitations of each type in terms of mission? Employment?

Quiz

TRUE OR FALSE

1. Most hospital governing boards include equal numbers of physicians and nurses.

2. Governance and management are different terms for the same set of responsibilities.

3. Directors and Operators liability insurance offers financial protection to board members who are named in a lawsuit as a result of their board activities.

4. Nonprofit organizations are termed nonprofit because they return financial profits to stockholders.

5. In addition to hospital care, the mission of academic medical centers includes university-based teaching and research-oriented colleges of medicine.

6. The term *span of control* refers to the number of services, people, or functions a leader is responsible for.

7. Ad hoc board committees are ongoing, permanent board structures.

8. The chief operating officer typically reports directly to the board.

9. Advisory boards hold fiduciary responsibility.

10. All health care organizations are governed by the same board structure.

MULTIPLE CHOICE

11. Critical access hospitals
   A. Must provide 24-hour emergency care 7 days a week
   B. Are reimbursed differently than hospitals that are not designated critical access hospitals
   C. Both A and B
   D. Neither A nor B

12. Ex officio board members
   A. Are board members by virtue of holding a particular job role or title
   B. Are always voting members of the board
   C. Both A and B
   D. Neither A nor B

13. The Sarbanes–Oxley Act
   A. Is an extension of Sherman antitrust legislation
   B. Dramatically changed the role of governing board quality committees
   C. Both A and B
   D. Neither A nor B

14. Board committees
   A. Typically have charters to define the role of the committee
   B. May include focus areas such as quality and finance
   C. Both A and B
   D. Neither A nor B

15. A governing board
   A. Typically sets the compensation level for the chief executive officer of an organization
   B. Is responsible for the hiring and, when necessary, firing of the chief executive officer
   C. Both A and B
   D. Neither A nor B

NOTE

1. Scenario is adapted from the overview of Enron authored by Sridharan, Dickes, and Royce Caines (2002).

REFERENCES

Anderson, R., Boumbulian, P., & Pickens, S. (2004). The role of US public hospitals in urban health. *Academic Medicine, 79*(12), 1162–1168.

Bader, B. (2010). Applying Sarbanes-Oxley to healthcare quality. *Great Boards* (Vol. 10). Potomac, MD: Bader and Associates Governance Consultants.

California Healthline. (2010, March 30). *Role of public hospitals unclear under health reform law.* Retrieved October 18, 2013, from http://www.californiahealthline.org

Congressional Budget Office (CBO). (2006). *Nonprofit hospitals and the provision of community benefit.* Retrieved July 16, 2014, from http://www.cbo.gov/sites/default/files/12-06-nonprofit.pdf

Horwitz, J. (2005). Making profit and providing care: Comparing nonprofit, for-profit, and governmental hospitals. *Health Affairs, 24*(3), 790–801. doi:10.1377/hlthaff.24.3.790

Institute of Medicine. (2010). *The future of nursing: Leading change, advancing health.* Washington, DC: National Academy of Sciences.

Legal Information Institute. (n.d.). *Fiduciary duty.* Retrieved August 9, 2014, from www.law.cornell.edu/wex/fiduciary_duty

Myers, S. (2008). A different voice: Nurses on the board. *Trustee, 6*(6), 10–14.

Nadler, D., Behan, B., & Nadler, M. (2006). *Building better boards: A blueprint for effective governance*. Hoboken, NJ: Wiley.

Rossiter, P. (2004). Supporting the audit committee after Sarbanes-Oxley: A practical guide. *Bank Accounting and Finance, 17*(5), 1–9.

Sridharan, U., Dickes, L., & Royce Caines, W. (2002). The social impact of business failure: Enron. *American Journal of Business, 17*(2), 11–22.

Sullivan, E. (2013). *Becoming influential: A guide for nurses* (2nd ed.). Boston, MA: Pearson.

Worth, M. (2013). *Nonprofit management: Principles and practices* (3rd ed.). Thousand Oaks, CA: Sage.

BUILDING SKILLS FOR BOARD MEMBERSHIP

FOLLOWING COMPLETION OF this chapter, you will be able to

- Identify personal skills and growth edges for board membership
- Describe board selection processes
- Determine board types of greatest personal interest and develop a plan toward board appointment
- Describe basic elements of organizational financial statements

Abby's twin sister, Emma, has just secured a position on the board of the regional home health agency. Abby states, "It is great you are there to represent nurses on the board!" Emma, who understands the governance responsibility to the mission, shakes her head, responding, "I don't represent nursing on the board. This is not a constituency board. Instead, I hope to exemplify what nurses can bring to a board."

ZEAL, ORGANIZATIONAL FIT, AND PHILANTHOPHY

Securing a position on a board is not about what the board can contribute to the board member's career, but instead is about what the individual can contribute to the board. At the same time, board membership builds important skills and connections and widens the board member's sphere of influence. It is also time-consuming. Thus, there are key dimensions to consider regarding becoming a board member. First, is the mission of the organization of interest? Zeal for the cause is a great mobilizer of both time and energy. This is important, as a committed board member will need both. Second, a commitment to a nonprofit board typically means not only time and energy but also at least some level of financial commitment to the organization on a yearly basis. Philanthropy, fund-raising for the institution, is an important responsibility of a board, and it is difficult to ask others to give to an organization if there is no commitment to philanthropy from 100% of the board members, demonstrated by giving personal funds to the organization. In other words, if the organization is not valuable enough for board members—who are the stewards and living logo for an organization—to give, why would anyone else?

Board Skill Mix

A second domain of exploration is an assessment of strengths and areas of potential impact and contribution. Every board needs members with complementary skills, and nurses offer valuable understanding of the delivery of health care. More important, however, the role of a governing board member is not to represent a constituency (e.g., nurses) on the board. Instead, each board member brings his or her knowledge, skills, and experience to serve the overall mission of the organization. Moreover, although nurses often know their own particular unit, specialty, or service delivery area, a board member is responsible to the whole organization, including finances. Most boards hold an orientation to acquaint board members with the range of efforts and activities of the board. Nevertheless, expanded understanding of the domains of governance responsibility will not only enhance effectiveness of the board member but also increase the likelihood of an appointment in the first place.

TYPES OF BOARD APPOINTMENTS

Self-Perpetuating Boards

Such appointments occur in two main ways. Some boards are *self-perpetuating boards*. In this model, existing board members identify potential new board members. This scenario creates obverse strengths and weaknesses. On the positive side, the board can shape itself to meet the demands of its responsibility, adding new skill sets to complement those of existing board members and address gaps or weaknesses in collective expertise. In contrast, under-represented groups will often continue to be underrepresented, as members naturally look among those they know or those with whom they share business or social interests, which can limit identifying a new population from which to draw potential board members (Worth, 2013). Nurses have traditionally been dramatically underrepresented in hospital boards, which tend to be self-perpetuating boards.

Appointed Boards

Other boards are *appointed boards*, with membership accessed through appointment by an official or authority who is not a direct part of the organization. This usually involves a political dimension, as the appointing authority is often composed of elected officials themselves. Many public universities, for example, are governed by boards that are appointed by the governor or through some other political process.

Elected Boards

A still different governance structure is that of *elected boards*. In the case of elected boards, as the name implies, the board members are elected by those being governed—the members of the organization. In this case, a level of visibility and perceived competency is necessary to be selected as a board member. Such visibility can be difficult for frontline staff, such as staff nurses, to obtain. Therefore, involvement in organizational committees and working groups is a valuable first step, both in skill building and network formation.

WHAT A GOVERNING BOARD IS NOT

Advisory Boards

It is important to reiterate that not all boards are governing boards, even if they hold the title of "board." Governing boards hold legal and fiduciary responsibility for the organization. *Advisory boards* serve important functions, providing insight, connections, and even philanthropic support, but do not hold legal, fiduciary responsibility. The leader in the organization does not report to such a board, but rather to someone else. As an example, a dean of a college of nursing may have an advisory board, but the dean herself reports to the provost/vice president (VP) for academic affairs, who in turn reports to the president of the university. The president, a role parallel to a chief executive officer (CEO), reports to a governing board.

Nevertheless, a role on an advisory board for an organization is also an important way to contribute and build board skills. There may a committee structure, although those committees would reflect the needs of the individual or organization that created the advisory board. Such a board is not responsible for quality and financial status of the organization and, correspondingly, these committees are not a typical part of the advisory board structure, but again—depending on the organization—both may exist on some advisory boards.

OTHER TYPES OF BOARDS

Constituency Boards

A still different variation of board type with a different route to board seat acquisition is *constituency boards*. In a constituency board, individuals represent a single agency, entity, or even a nation. In such a model, the board member has the responsibility to promulgate the views of the entity that he or she represents, rather than putting that identity aside to address the collective mission. The role of constituency board members must include a mechanism by which the representative can garner the views of the constituency group as well as report back to them. Therefore, unlike a typical nonprofit board role where the individual board member uses his or her own best judgment in the organization's overall best interest, constituency board membership involves substantial, ongoing communication with constituency members. An example of a constituency board would be one in which the members represent the nurses' association, medical association, physical therapy association, small businesses, and so on. Such board members may have conflicting agendas, as often the representative board member is also lobbyist for that organization and has the responsibility to work for the best interests of its members, including their financial well-being. This is unlike the previously detailed nonprofit governing boards, in which the responsibility includes putting personal interests aside.

Regulatory Boards

A regulatory board is not a governing board, constituency board, or advisory board. Instead, a regulatory board has the responsibility for the enforcement of a particular *statute* or law to ensure compliance with that law, typically via *administrative rules,* in which the administrative rule is the more detailed policies and procedures. The regulatory board, sometimes called *regulatory authority* or *regulatory body,* is a governmental entity that has the responsibility for oversight in the best interest of the public. An example would be a state *board of nursing.* Such a body's responsibility is to protect the public, not to represent nurses or nursing. State regulatory boards are typically appointed by the state governor in a process that varies by state and by the particular regulatory body. Health care is a highly regulated function in society, and regulatory bodies may oversee Certificates of Need and hospital budgets, as just two examples, while a board of nursing oversees nursing practice and education to assure that the public is protected. Importantly, the board of nursing is not accountable to nursing per se, nor does it represent nurses in the same way as a nursing association, but instead is accountable to the public for safe nursing practice.

In many regulatory boards, the *executive director* of the board is a staff person who is hired by and reports to the board, similar to the CEO in a governing board. Again, to underscore, unlike a governing board, there is no board fiduciary responsibility. Instead, there is a responsibility to ensure the execution of the state law. Take a moment to review the process for appointment to the board of nursing in your state by viewing the board website. That will give you a sense of how nurses are appointed to one regulatory body in your setting.

BUILDING THE SKILL SET FOR BOARD MEMBERSHIP

There is no clear-cut set of strategies or experiences that lead to board membership, but there are skills and competencies that you can foster to be ready to comfortably seek or be ready to accept a board position. Test your skill set for board membership and determine your strengths and growth edges using the following skills checklist.

Skill 1: I Understand How Meetings Are Run and the Protocols Around Rules of Order, Such as Robert's Rules of Order or the Modern Rules of Order

In some boards, the culture is such that meetings are run loosely or at least more loosely than a full formal protocol or set of rules would demand. Other boards maintain strict attention to protocol. Although the best way to have a sense of the culture in a particular group is to participate in different meetings as an active member, here are a few guidelines.

Typically there is a *chair* and *members* of the board. The chair, often with input from management or other board members, develops the *meeting agenda*. This agenda, inclusive of date, location, times, and items for discussion and vote, is distributed prior to the meeting, typically via e-mail (see Box 10.1 for an example of an agenda). The details of time and location are critical. Different organizations have different bylaws on the length of time before the meeting that the agenda must be distributed, but a common time frame is 1 to 2 weeks. Certain critical voting elements may have to be *warned* of at least a month prior to the meeting, warning meaning informing the board of the upcoming vote on a particular issue. This sort of structure would be common in a body like a university senate, in which many members need to be assembled and, thus, must have sufficient notice, not only to be sure that they can attend but also to obtain input from the constituencies they represent about an issue under consideration.

CALL TO ORDER

The chair calls the meeting to order and "runs the meeting." A *permanent chair* differs from a *convening chair*, whose role is simply to pull the group together and thus has a different level of power and influence and, indeed, a different role.

ESTABLISHMENT OF A QUORUM

Most boards, and other groups such as a university senate, require that there be a predefined *quorum*, a proportion or percentage of the membership that must be present, if a vote is to occur. The proportion of the group needed to constitute a quorum is typically established in the organizational *bylaws*. You can think of bylaws as a set of organizational rules.

Thus, the first order of business is to establish if there is a quorum of members in attendance. The absence of a quorum is unlikely in major boards, but some smaller, new, or struggling boards may suffer from attendance issues among board members. If there is no quorum in attendance, those attending can decide to hold the meeting for the purpose of discussion, but no voting can occur. Or the group may decide to reschedule. The quorum criterion is also a necessary aspect of committee meetings, and small committees are more likely to be plagued by quorum issues because the absence of one or two members may mean a majority of members are not in attendance.

Box 10.1

Sample Agenda

Pleasant Valley Hospital Board of Trustee Meeting
Date: April 15, 2015
Time: 1:00 p.m.
Location: Pleasant Valley Hospital Board Room A, 10th Floor, West
Corridor
1353 Fictitious Lane
Anytown, USA

1. Call to order—Jane Smith, Chair	1:00 p.m.
2. Review of previous minutes—Jane Smith, Chair	1:01 p.m.
3. Chair's report—Jane Smith, Chair	1:05 p.m.
4. CEO's report—David Hernandez, CEO, Pleasant Valley Hospital	1:15 p.m.
5. Standing committee reports	
A. Audit Committee: Peter Smith, Audit Committee Chair	1:25 p.m.
B. Finance Committee: Aki Chang, Finance Committee Chair	1:35 p.m.
C. Planning Committee: Jada Kennedy, Planning Committee Chair	1:45 p.m.
D. Quality Committee: Xavier Gonzalez, Quality Committee Chair	1:55 p.m.
6. Old business	
A. Union negotiations: Lamar Jones, Vice President for Human Resources	2:05 p.m.
B. Quality institute planning: Lakshmi Chada, Chief Quality Officer	2:30 p.m.
7. New business	
ACO acquisition: David Hernandez, CEO, & Jada Kennedy, Planning Committee Chair	3:00 p.m.
8. Adjournment. Jane Smith, Chair	4:00 p.m.

Note: All names represent fictitious characters
ACO, accountable care organization; CEO, chief executive officer.

APPROVAL OF MINUTES FROM THE PREVIOUS MEETING

Once the quorum is established, the next line of business is approval of previous minutes. Although this may seem like a perfunctory issue, these minutes become the permanent record of board action. In the event of a legal challenge to board action or inquiry of any type, the minutes are a key reference. As a board member, it is wise to read minutes carefully, be sure they are complete and correct, and if not, to offer *corrections and additions*. A motion and second to accept the corrected minutes will likely follow. Also, a member who was not at the meeting should abstain from this vote, as it is not possible for them to assess the accuracy of minutes for a meeting they did not attend.

Open Meeting Laws

Some public bodies function under an *open meeting law,* meaning all business except personnel or contract issues must be open to the public, including the minutes being open and individuals being free to choose to attend a meeting as a spectator. Such meetings may be videotaped, creating a permanent public record. The written minutes are then often terse, as the full record is available on videotape.

CHAIR'S REPORT AND CEO'S REPORT

At this point, the protocol in different boards varies. A common approach is for a *chair's report*, updating the board, followed by a *CEO's report*. Alternatively, these may be previously provided in written form and this time used simply for questions about the written materials.

COMMITTEE REPORTS

Committee reports, provided by the committee chairs, are next. If there are recommendations that come from the committee, they are vetted by the full board at that time. Recommendations coming from a committee do not require a seconded motion for discussion leading to a vote. This, of course, makes sense: The recommendation has already been, in essence, supported by at least two people, which is what is needed for a motion and a second. The full board then discusses committee recommendations, and a vote is taken. Prior to a vote, several actions can take place.

Voting Process

A *friendly amendment* is a recommended change to a motion or recommendation that is in keeping with the original motion, but offers some refinement or small change. The original maker of the motion or recommendation must agree to the friendly amendment, as must the individual who offered the second to the original motion. If so, the vote is on the new language. A more formal means to alter a motion or recommendation is with a motion for an amendment. This, if moved and seconded, is then discussed and voted on. If it is approved, the discussion then returns to *main motion as amended*. If it is not approved, the discussion returns to the original motion. In either case, at the conclusion of discussion, there is a vote. If there is a great number of unanswered questions or a conflict, a member may make a motion to *table* the item, which means to put the issue aside and not vote on it at that time. If seconded, there would be a vote on tabling the item. If the motion to table is supported, the item is not further discussed at that time, although a plan for further information gathering or to revisit it at some point in the future is common. A timetable or set date to return to the item may also be required. If the motion to table the item is not supported, the conversation returns to the motion under discussion.

A still different action prior to the vote is to *call the question*. This typically happens if there is protracted conversation about a motion. If the question is called, a mistake typically made is for the chair to immediately cease all conversation and go to the vote on the main motion (or main motion as amended, if that is the motion under discussion). Instead, the correct protocol is that when the question is called, and if it is seconded, there must be a vote on calling the question, that is, a vote on whether or not discussion should cease. If the motion and second to call the question are supported by majority vote, discussion does cease and a vote is taken on the main motion, or the main motion as amended, depending on what previously ensued. If the vote to call the question does not pass, discussion continues.

Standing Reports, Old Business, and New Business

As noted in Box 10.1, standing committee reports are typically followed by a discussion of old and new business, which may also present items requiring a vote. State regulatory boards may have a mandatory period for public comment and a process by which the public can comment before a board can act on an item, meaning that no item can be introduced and voted on in the same meeting. Regulatory boards are discussed in greater detail later in this chapter.

Action Item or Educational Session?

In addition to meetings including *action items,* or those needing a vote, most boards hold educational sessions. These may be a part of full board meetings, or the board may alternate *action meetings* with *educational meetings.* Clearly, board membership requires a level of communication between and among group members as well as the public. This will be the next item on the skill set checklist.

Skill 2: I Can Speak in a Clear and Direct Way in Public, and My Appearance Creates Confidence in My Message and Abilities

This skill may come naturally to you. If not, it is a skill that can be practiced. Many colleges and universities require graduates to demonstrate some level of an oral proficiency competency and offer courses to teach "public speaking," as it is often called. Such courses offer an ideal time to hone skills with guided feedback. A more independent way to augment your public speaking skills is to videotape yourself on either a phone or a medium like YouTube. If you are practicing on YouTube and do not want this publicly disseminated, be sure to select the setting as "private." Self-taping provides an unparalleled way to identify strengths and growth edges. Self-query questions as you review the presentation include the following:

- Is my manner direct? Confident? Trustworthy? Do I have any mannerisms that distract from these important qualities, such as eye shifting or eye rolling? Do the "uhs" or "likes" get in the way of the message?
- Does my visual appearance inspire confidence in the audience I am trying to connect with? Remember that your physical appearance can help forge a form of overlap between yourself and the group. Thus, your clothing, accessories, and makeup are extremely important. There is an almost instantaneous impression based on appearance, which is closely followed and informed by language, tone, and grammar: Who are you saying you are, with your visual messages?

Finally, while it is important to be yourself, recall that there are different elements of your skills and abilities that you can bring to the forefront in different settings that may either be more or less readily accepted, based on appearance. If, for example, you are meeting with a group of homeless adolescents, bonding would likely be facilitated if you *did not* arrive in the sort of polished business attire that would be the norm for corporate or nonprofit boardrooms. Conversely, wearing jeans, shirts without ties, and other casual wear may not inspire the desired impression in a group of business and political leaders. The local culture also makes a difference in what constitutes *appropriate professional attire*. In a meeting at a small nonprofit in a very rural remote area, casual, comfortable shoes may be appropriate, but out of place—marking you as an outsider—if that meeting were in Manhattan. Nurses sometimes attend meeting in scrubs, as do physicians. Although this can reinforce the image of the practicing clinician, it may be inappropriate or at the least not optimal for a board-level meeting. As Suzanne Gordon (2005) notes, nurses undermine their own authority by "showing up in what looks like pajamas," particularly when these scrubs have images on them such as animals. A trusted mentor can help you navigate these various issues. Also be sure to observe board politics and power dynamics for clues on how to best present your message so you will be heard and taken seriously.

Skill 3: I Understand Financial Operations and Financial Reports

This is a particularly important competency for governing board members because one of the key responsibilities of the board is to provide and oversee the organization's budget. It is critical to understand, however, that this approval and oversight occurs at a high level; the board members do not determine individual expenses. Instead, a strategic vision is developed by leadership in collaboration with other members of the organization, typically with performance metrics. These may be approved by the board, but the institutional budget may be considered the living strategic plan. It details the organization's priorities by illustrating where and how financial resources are allocated. Moreover, many financial allocations translate to human resources, for example, the salaries of individuals doing the work of the organization, including nurses. Therefore, attention to the distribution of resources between human and material resources illustrated on the financial report is warranted.

WHAT ABOUT FINANCIAL STATEMENTS?

The organization's financial statements will first be vetted by the finance committee, and only then reviewed by the full board. They are organized in a standard manner, with assets listed first and liabilities second. The *budget to actual* is typically included, as is a comparison to a previous year-to-date budget, to be discussed in greater detail later in this chapter. Negative numbers are shown in parentheses or may literally be illustrated in red ink; hence the colloquialism of *being in the red.*

SALARIES AND FRINGE BENEFITS

As a human resource–intensive industry, health care organizations typically employ a large number of individuals. This is reflected in budget sheets as salaries. Note also, however, that fringe benefits such as health insurance and retirement contributions are a notable portion of a budget. Using a hypothetical employee with a salary of $100,000/year, for example, an organization whose fringe rate is 30% would need to have budgeted—and have available—$130,000/year for compensation for that employee. The largest portion of fringe benefits is typically health insurance.

WHAT DOES THE TERM "DAYS CASH ON HAND" MEAN AND WHY IS IT IMPORTANT?

A second key background concept important to all organizational types is *days cash on hand.* This concept is similar to a personal checking account for meeting regular, ongoing expenses, and a cushion is needed to ensure that the organization can meet ongoing obligations—paying its nurses, for example.

WHAT ARE BOND RATING AND BOND COVENANTS?

Not only is days cash on hand important in *making payroll,* that is, having the financial resources to pay employees and other regular expenses, it is one element that determines an organization's *bond rating* and impacts *bond covenants.* The term bond rating refers to an organization's *credit worthiness,* while the term bond covenant refers to a set of rules or parameters around a borrowing arrangement. Bond rating will impact how much an organization can borrow and how much it costs the organization in terms of interest rating. An organization may need funds to expand the physical plant (buildings) of a hospital, for example, and higher credit rating enables the organization to borrow money at a lower interest rate and thus lower long-term debt. In the United States, there are three common raters, Moody's Investors Services, Standard and Poor's, and Fitch, and a rating for an organization may differ slightly among them. An organization that has obtained bonds for some sort of project must abide by the previously noted bond covenants or rules of the borrowing arrangement. Days cash on hand is a key financial "vital sign" in an organization, as is the amount of *long term-debt* and the ratio of *debt to total capital* (see Box 10.2 for analogous simple, everyday examples of these concepts). This latter concept is sometimes termed *debt-to-cap* or *D/C ratio*. This ratio is simply an index of the amount of debt compared to other assets; you can think about this as the loans-to-assets ratio.

WHAT DOES "BUDGET TO ACTUAL" MEAN?

When attending a board meeting or a meeting of the finance committee, organizations also provide a written report of *budget to actual revenues* and *budget to actual liabilities*. Although these may seem like very foreign terms,

---

Box 10.2
Defining Common Financial Terms

Long-term debt can be differentiated from short-term debt in the following manner. Imagine you decide to buy a new dining room set, and you are able to obtain a 12-month loan from the furniture company. This is short-term debt, in contrast to, for example, a home mortgage in which the loan for your home will be paid with a monthly amount over 30 consecutive years. The mortgage constitutes long-term debt.

Debt-to-capitalization ratios can be conceptualized in the following contrasting situations, the first with a low debt-to-capitalization ratio and the second with a high debt-to-capitalization ratio. Imagine you owe $10,000 on a new car valued at $30,000, and you own a fully paid-off $300,000 home. In this case, you have very little debt in relationship to assets. Contrast this with a situation in which you owe $10,000 on your car, which is worth only $12,000, but also have $100,000 in student loans and no other assets.

It is a bit more complicated in health care, of course, but these scenarios illustrate the basic ideas. Which of the two individuals above would you rather be? If you were a bank, which one would you rather give a loan to? Similarly, organizations with lower long-term debt and a low debt-to-capitalization ratio are in better financial health and considered more creditworthy.

---

these concepts are actually very familiar to you in your everyday life. You can consider these terms parallel to the following statements in your own household. Budget to actual revenue: "I thought I was going to have x amount of money coming in (budgeted revenue), but I actually have y amount of money coming in (actual revenue)." Budget to actual liabilities: "I thought I was going to have z amount of money I would need to pay out (budgeted liability), but I actually have q amount of money I need to pay out (actual liabilities)." The difference between x and y is called a *variance,* as is the difference between z and q.

Obviously, an organization that consistently has more actual liabilities than actual revenue is not in sound financial health. Remember also that budgeted revenues are *predictions* of what an organization believes it will receive, and these estimates may never be perfectly on target with actual, no matter how skillful the organization. Some variance is expected, just not dramatic variance.

What Sorts of Circumstances Create Budget Variances?

Revenue in a health care organization includes things like Medicare, Medicaid, and commercial insurance reimbursement, among others. When an organization sets its budget based on an expected rate of Medicaid reimbursement, for example, and that state later responds to budget shortfall by cutting Medicaid reimbursement rates midyear, that actual revenue will be lower than initially budgeted. (The term for this sort of change is *rescission,* which means cutting out or repealing something that was previously approved.) Variance can also be related to how many health services people are using. *Lower than expected volumes*—that is, the amount of services given to patients in an organization—will result in a lower actual revenue than budgeted in an organization receiving fee-for-service reimbursement. A variance can also be created following expenditures or costs that are higher or lower than expected. If, for example, there is an extremely harsh winter, actual heating costs (noted in the budget sheet under the term *utilities* and inclusive of other utilities such as electricity) may be much higher than budgeted. Conversely, an unexpectedly mild winter may result in lower-than-budgeted utility expenses. The important concept to take away here is that, unlike how the term budget is used more commonly, the "budget" of an organization is a plan, whereas "actuals" are what actually happens. Finally, liabilities in a health care organization will include things like salaries for staff and payment on debts. Take a moment to locate and review these financial reports on your institution's website.

WHAT ABOUT PAYER MIX?

The items just discussed are common to all organizations, but there are financial elements (discussed in earlier chapters) that are unique to health care and merit reconsideration as you review financial reports. Key among these are *payer mix*, the proportion of revenue from commercial insurers, Medicare, and Medicaid; as well the proportion of *bad debt* and *charity care*, which represents charges that are not collected (see Box 10.3). As detailed in previous chapters, cost, charges, and reimbursement are not the same. Therefore,

---

Box 10.3
What Is the Difference Between Bad Debt and Charity Care?

Bad debt and charity care are both ways in which hospitals report care given to those who are uninsured or underinsured. Hospitals typically have a policy about how this care is charged; for example, they may set the charge at the Medicare rate rather than the much higher commercial insurance rate. They may also work with uninsured individuals to see if they are indeed eligible for some sort of coverage such as Medicaid. Even so, some individuals will not have coverage, meaning that the facility is providing uncompensated care. This charity care is known upon admission, and the magnitude of charity care is carefully monitored because some states provide reimbursement to hospitals for some portion of the charity care, and charity care is part of a financial formula that reimburses hospitals that serve a high proportion of uninsured individuals and Medicaid patients. This is called a Disproportionate Share Payment (DSP; Jackson, Derose, Chiesa, & Escarce, 2014), commonly voiced as "dish" payment. There is also a DSP formula for Medicare, which was modified with the passage of the Affordable Care Act.

Bad debt refers to a different phenomenon and basically refers to individuals who do not pay their bill after receiving services. Unlike charity care, where the situation is known up-front, bad debt is discovered after the treatment. These persons may be insured, but have a high deductible, for example.

If the Affordable Care Act goal of having all insured becomes a reality, institutions should, over time, provide an increasingly diminishing proportion of charity care. If many individuals and families select higher deductible plans such as Bronze, however, bad debt may increase.

---

organizations may look similar in terms of cost and charges, but be compensated at very different levels based on payer mix. Again, take a moment to search the website of a local health care organization and see if you can locate and read a financial statement to further acquaint yourself with these aspects of financial operations and reports.

NEXT STEPS

In summary, three major areas of strength that complement your clinical and nursing practice knowledge will help you access a board position. These are being meeting savvy, good presentation of self, and financial acumen. Create a list of your strengths and gaps. Then, if possible, review it with a colleague who will give you an honest critique. Then, develop a plan to fill those gaps.

Thought Questions

1. How do board member roles vary on different kinds of boards? Why are there these differences?

2. What strengths would you bring to a governing board? Regulatory board? Advisory board?

3. What is appropriate professional attire for participation in a hospital board meeting?

4. Define the following key terms:

Action item	Constituency board
Action meeting	Convening chair
Administrative rules	Corrections and additions to minutes
Appointed board	
Appropriate professional attire	Days cash on hand
	Education meeting
CEO's report	Elected boards
Chair's report	Main motion

Main motion as amended   Self-perpetuating board

Open meeting law   Warned vote

Quorum

Exercises

1. Role-play a governing board meeting. Assign peers and yourself to different governing board roles and hold a mock board meeting. Be sure to have the chair prepare the agenda in advance and have voting items.

2. Attend an open meeting of the state board of nursing or other state regulatory board.

3. Does your nursing program have an advisory board? Are there students on it? Or is there a student advisory board, in which students provide insight to the dean? If so, who are these students, and how did they get appointed?

4. Obtain the bylaws of your college or university or local hospital (try the institution's website). What do they say about a quorum? What other rules are identified?

5. Most hospital board meetings include a session for the public. Attend and report back to peers on what you observed. What financial terms did you understand? Which ones were confusing to you?

Quiz

TRUE OR FALSE

1. In self-perpetuating boards, existing board members identify potential new members.

2. One strength of a self-perpetuating board is the capacity to easily expand board membership to underrepresented groups.

3. Typically, a quorum of board members is needed for board action items that require a vote.

4. Another term for statute is administrative rule.

5. Another term for statute is law.

6. Similar to a chief executive officer, the executive director is hired by and reports to the board.

7. Charity care differs from bad debt in that care that will be charity is known by the institution at the time of admission, whereas bad debt will not be known by the institution until the individual fails to pay whatever remains on the bill.

8. The financial term debt-to-cap ratio is synonymous with the term days cash on hand.

9. The term bond covenant refers to rules that are part of an organization's borrowing agreement.

10. An organization's deemed credit worthiness is identified by its bond rating.

MULTIPLE CHOICE

11. Different types of boards appoint new members using different approaches. These include
    A. Election
    B. Appointment
    C. Both A and B
    D. Neither A nor B

12. Regulatory boards
    A. Represent the interests of shareholders
    B. Hold fiduciary responsibility
    C. Both A and B
    D. Neither A nor B

13. Which is a type of board in which members are typically appointed by a political entity such as the state governor?
    A. Governing board
    B. Regulatory board
    C. Advisory board
    D. All of the above

14. The type of board that is most likely to be responsible for enforcement of a statute is a:
    A. Governing board
    B. Regulatory board
    C. Advisory board
    D. All of the above

15. What constitutes appropriate professional attire?
    A. May vary depending on the audience, venue, or group
    B. May be discerned with the help of a trusted mentor
    C. Both A and B
    D. Neither A nor B

REFERENCES

Gordon, S. (2005). *Nursing against the odds: How health care cost cutting, media stereotypes, and medical hubris undermine nurses and patient care.* Ithaca, NY: Cornell University Press.

Jackson, C. A., Derose, K. P., Chiesa, J., & Escarce, J. J. (2014). *Distribution of uncompensated care. Hospital Care for the Insured in Miami-Dade County.* Santa Monica, CA: RAND Corporation. Retrieved August 30, 2014, from http://www.rand.org/content/dam/rand/pubs/monograph_reports/MR1522/MR1522.ch3.pdf

Worth, M. (2013). *Nonprofit management: Principles and practices* (3rd ed.). Thousand Oaks, CA: Sage.

11

APPLYING HEALTH ECONOMICS TO INFLUENCE HEALTH CARE THROUGH STATE AND FEDERAL POLICY FORMATION

FOLLOWING COMPLETION OF this chapter, you will be able to

- Describe the policy process
- Detail points of influence in policy formation
- Explore the unique contribution of nurses in policy formation
- Develop a learning agenda for enhancing personal political influence

I see clinicians and other people who work in health care as incredibly committed, really trying to do the right thing. They are advocating for people's health on a daily basis. Yet they are not always adept about policy because it is not a world they travel in. So I would like to see more clinicians integrated into the policy process—in part because they have such a rich voice.

—Julie Sochalski, in an interview by Pulcini (2014, p. 19)

Two hundred years ago, women did not have the right to vote. Neither did people of color. Today, all citizens, including nurses, have the opportunity to influence policy in meaningful ways. Nurses have held positions in Congress, state legislatures, and other prominent positions. However, a nurse does not need to run for political office to be influential. Numbering nearly 3 million (Health Resources and Services Administration, 2013), nurses have a collective opportunity to be a substantial force in health care policy, health policy, and economic and social policy writ large. Too few nurses, however, seize this opportunity. Arguably, nurses may subconsciously view their role as a private relationship between patients and their families and themselves, the nurses. In the same vein, nurses studied nursing in college, not political science or law, alternative pathways that might have indicated an intention to become active in politics. Yet even one small policy change may impact thousands or even millions of lives and offers a profound means of beneficence. What follows, therefore, is a dissection of the political process, with suggestions for active involvement at various scales and levels of intensity. After all, *politics* means, literally, *the work of the people*, given that the Latin origin of the word "poli" means "many." Nothing could be more compatible with nursing than policy formation, offering broad solutions to societal problems through policy and politics.

WAYS OF INFLUENCE

Voting

A foundational and basic way to have influence is at the ballot box: vote! As simple as it seems, many American do not vote. As previously noted, a mere 100 years ago, four to five generations ago, women did not have the right to vote—they did not win the right to vote until 1920—whereas "race, color, or previous condition of servitude" were addressed 50 years earlier, in 1870, with the passage of the 15th Amendment. These victories were hard won. As a first step toward influence, register to vote...and vote!

Political Campaigns

A next level is to become involved with a political campaign. Offering time for a worthy candidate or a cause is an excellent way to demystify the political process. Activities can range from preparing social media to stuffing envelopes, dropping flyers off door to door, fund-raising, or working on the *get-out-the-vote effort*—activities designed to assure that supporters actually arrive at the ballot box. No activity is so small as to be insignificant. What if time is short? Do not underestimate the power of even a small contribution to a campaign. In the world of politics, money matters. Money materializes in the world as human and material resources. Contributing time, money, or both is a valuable way to further a cause.

Political Action Committees

Financial resources go further when they are merged with those of like-minded others. *Political action committees,* or *PACs,* offer a way of pooling funds with others. Political action group funds may support particular candidates or causes, so it is important to carefully consider which groups to join. Key questions to ask before providing financial support include the following:

1. What are the views or platform of the group?
2. Do you agree with these views and resulting strategies, or are you—through your dues or additional PAC contributions—supporting something that is not aligned with your interests and ideals?

Lobbyists

Many organizations fund a *lobbyist.* A lobbyist is an individual who actively works to influence policymakers to take a particular view or vote a particular way. At a state level, nursing organizations may not be sufficiently financed to support a lobbyist at the statehouse full time, whereas better resourced organizations such as hospital and medical associations employ lobbyists who become part of the trusted fabric of state politics. This creates an unfortunate power differential in political influence that can be difficult for nursing to overcome. The many different nursing groups, sometimes with conflicting views and messages, may also be confusing to policymakers. A unified message or set of messages from the various groups representing nurses and nursing is warranted whenever possible.

Is All Advocacy Lobbying?

What is the difference between being a lobbyist versus simply advocating for an issue? Although there are some similarities, there are important distinctions. *Lobbying* is activity to influence legislators or federal policymakers

---

Box 11.1

What Is a Bill Draft?

Long before something becomes a law, it exists in earlier forms. First, there needs to be an idea, and this idea is then drafted into a bill or a preliminary version of what the law might look like.

---

to vote a particular way on a piece of legislation. *Direct lobbying* is done by a registered lobbyist who is officially representing the views of a particular group, frequently having been hired to do so. The process by which to register as a lobbyist varies by state, but an individual cannot lobby without taking the appropriate actions that include a process, forms, and fees. Typically, there are also strict ethical guidelines regarding gifts from lobbyists to policymakers. Professional lobbyists may also analyze regulatory proposals or drafts of proposed bills (see Box 11.1) to inform the organization of the potential impact of proposed legislative action. Take a moment to review lobbying guidelines on your state government's website.

LOBBYING AS OFFICIAL AUTHORITY TO REPRESENT A GROUP VIEW

In summary, active lobbying signifies *official authority* to represent the group. A responsibility of a lobbyist for a state nurses' association is to represent the interests and view of that group, which are not necessarily the lobbyist's own. In some controversial areas, patient-directed dying, for example, the organization may poll members to determine what stance they want officially represented. Alternatively, based on stated values or following polling of a group, the official organizational stance may be to take no position. Individual members of groups can always be in contact with policymakers representing their own views, but they cannot simply hold themselves up as representatives of the group's collective position.

GRASSROOTS LOBBYING

Conversely, *grassroots lobbying* is the mobilization of individuals within a group to influence legislation. Such groups may promulgate a *call to action* suggesting that individuals contact their state or federal policymakers to support, oppose, or amend a particular bill. As a citizen, of course, you can contact policymakers at any time, with or without such an action prompt. Nevertheless, alignment with a group that continually monitors federal and/or state legislation and promulgates calls to action is a helpful way to keep track of the myriad of constantly shifting details that characterize the political process without having to navigate it alone.

HOW TO CONTACT POLICYMAKERS

Gabriella is amazed at how easy it was to influence legislation to increase the student loan repayment program in her state! The nursing student association forwarded an action alert, and Gabriella took a deep breath and called her state representative who, incidentally, is on the committee that reviewed the bill draft. Gabriella initially left a phone message to detail her perspective. Representative Smith then asked Gabriella to testify to the committee on the issue of student debt load and the value of loan repayment as a state workforce retention strategy.

Obviously, to take a step like Gabriella did, it is critical to know who to call. Do you know who represents you in the House and Senate? Please take a moment to identify your district, representatives, and senators at both the state and national level. This is essential, basic knowledge for political influence.

Is It a Good Idea or a Good Idea That Should Become a Law?

With this knowledge, you can now influence policy in a number of ways. If there is an issue you would like to see become a law, first ponder if it is a good idea or a good idea that should become a law. This is an important distinction. Not every good idea should be a law, as laws have enforcement requirements as well as other costs. If you decide on the latter, it is helpful to first explore if a bill on this issue had previously been introduced and trace what happened to that bill. This creates an "in the know" starting platform. If you continue to believe state legislation should be proposed, you can contact your state senator or representative and ask him or her to sponsor a bill. Recall that these individuals are elected to represent you. That is the whole idea of a representative form of government. Alternatively, you may bond with like-minded others and create a collective strategy for approaching legislative action. Coalitions of interested parties can bring issues to the attention of policymakers. Unusual alliances are particularly powerful. Ponder, for example, the difference between students and universities promoting loan repayment and these groups reinforced by the hospital association and statewide chamber of commerce. The broader nature of the latter creates political momentum. Similarly, nursing and consumer groups that together advocate for a policy change are in a much more powerful political position than when either group is advocating in isolation.

Phone Calls to Policymakers

If instead there is a current bill or item of a bill that you strongly support or oppose, a phone call is very effective. Letters are also effective, but know that at the federal level this is inefficient, and there may be a long delay between when you send the letter and when it is received. This is because land mail is extensively screened following the anthrax scare a few years back; a phone call or e-mail is better, or visit the federal staff in person, either in your Congress member's state office or when you are in Washington, DC.

Health Staff to Federal Policymakers

Do you know who is staffing your federal representatives and senators in the area of health and health-related issues? Do you know where the state offices of these Congress members are located? Organized meetings with staff members can be a powerful tool, provided the message is clear and well organized. These individuals work for your representatives and senators, and again, these representatives of the people cannot represent you if they do not know your thoughts. They depend on all of their constituents for reelection, so do not conclude that they are powerful and you are not; you have the power of your own voice—your vote—and your connection with coalitions of similar-minded individuals and groups.

Legislative Committees

Laws are like sausages—it is best not to see them being made (attributed to Otto Von Bismarck).[1]

Senators and representatives serve on committees, and much of the "hammering out" work is done there. As the famous Bismarck quote illustrates, like sausage, what initially goes into a bill draft may look very different from the final product, the bill that receives enough votes to be passed into law. Amendments, deletions, and additions are common. A bill may change so much in the process that something you once supported, you may now oppose. Thus, it is important to follow a bill of interest through the entire legislative process. Moreover, sometimes competing bills are introduced, again illustrating why fully engaged lobbyists and government relations staff can be so valuable to an organization or cause.

If a bill of interest has been introduced, it is first reviewed in committee, with testimony on the bill heard by the committee. A committee is a sort of working group that delves more deeply into the details of a domain of interest and develops expertise by which it can shepherd issues to the full legislative body. Committees offer a form of specialization, for example, in areas such as health, environment, and education, to name just a few. Other committees deal with the actual funding of bills, for example, the appropriations committee or—at the national level—the House Ways and Means Committee. Take a moment to review the website for your state governance structure as well as the parallel information at the national level (www .house.gov and www.senate.gov).

INFLUENCING AT THE COMMITTEE LEVEL

Who to contact? If the chair of the committee is in your district, contacting the chair of the committee with your input is a particularly effective strategy; committee chairs set agendas and tones, an explicit and implicit form of influence, respectively. Understandably, they want to have and keep your vote! Also look to see if any of your representatives serve on key committees. Yet, the committee chair is not the only avenue. Committee members are also key influencers during the committee review process.

TIMING MATTERS

Timing matters! If the bill is still in committee, contacting committee members is most effective. If it has gone to the floor for a vote, then it is very effective to contact whomever represents you. State your position clearly and succinctly. Also know that in small states, representatives and senators are largely without full staff support. Thus, if there is an area in which you are an expert, a short list of *talking points* may aid the policymaker if he or she wishes to articulate that position on the floor of the House or Senate. Also, note *crossover* in the "How a Bill Becomes a Law" diagram (see Figure 11.1). Committee hearings and votes happen on one side, say the House, then mid-session, switch to the Senate, and it starts all over again as a bill to be considered by that body.

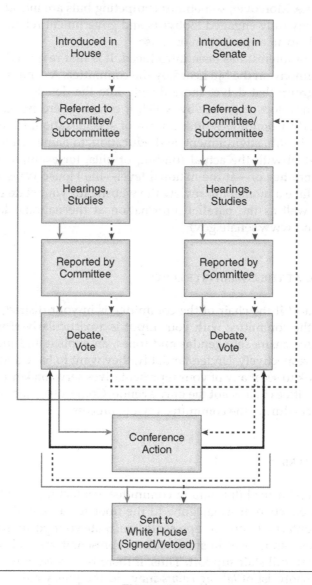

Figure 11.1
How a bill becomes a law.

MAINTAINING A CONNECTION WITH POLICYMAKERS TO INFLUENCE HEALTH AND HEALTH CARE

A sustained connection with a policymaker or policymakers can result in the nurse and nursing agendas having considerable influence throughout the legislative process, from bill drafting and committee hearings to full chamber review. Nursing interests may be forgotten not out of malice, but simply because nurses are not visible in the process. In many states, the absence of a constant nursing presence at the statehouse results in comparative invisibility. In such cases, identification of additional stakeholders and subsequent coalition building is a valuable way to foster a nursing presence. Finally, nursing involvement in health policy may be focused on health care, but activities directed toward the broader social determinants of health are a worthy contribution as well. Nurses are credible to the public, and advocating for policies that do not directly benefit nurses adds additional credibility to the cause under review.

OVERCOMING IMPEDIMENTS TO INVOLVEMENT

Tensions With Powerful Others

Des Jardin (2001a) suggests that nurse involvement in the political process is hampered by more than just a lack of knowledge about the process. Nurses may feel an inconsistency between the goals of professional nursing and those of the institutional and physician sector of health care. A contemporary illustration is the continuing tensions between organized medicine and authority roles for nurses, for example, the American Medical Association chastising The Joint Commission for not mandating that physicians must be the heads of medical homes, in contrast to the stance promulgated by the American Association of Nurse Practitioners, which stated: "A patient's needs should determine who leads a team and leadership should not be 'defined by a profession'" (Robeznieks, 2014, para 15). (At the time of this writing, The Joint Commission has continued its long-standing position that nurse-led care teams can qualify for its primary care medical home certification.) A second example is the potential tension between an employing hospital that does not support legislated limits on nurse–patient ratios and a nurse who does. It is important to recall that an organization such as the American Medical Association or American Hospital Association exists to support the interests of physicians and hospitals, respectively, which may or may not be aligned with the interests of nurses or society at large. As the nurse in these crosshairs, these potential schisms are easily reconciled from an ethical perspective: Any and all potential or real conflicts of interest must be resolved in the best interest of the patient.

Stereotypical Images of Nurses and Policy: Do Nurses Internalize Politically Powerless Self-Images?

Des Jardin (2001b) also suggests that stereotypical images of nurse as mother, servant, religious symbol, and military angel such as Florence Nightingale may not only be held by society, but internalized by nurses. Gordon (2005) has argued that the "virtue script" and complex adaptation of nurses to assuring deference to physicians artfully conceals the genuine mastery of health care by nurses. Moreover, these emotional and societal stances do not encourage the acquisition of voice and comfort with controversy, yet controversy is inherent in the political process. Similarly, Summers and Summers (2010) suggest that media images of nurses as backdrops, gurney pushers, and agents in romantic plots devalue and dismiss nurses. Again, the extent to which nurses internalize these images is difficult to estimate. Nevertheless, such images matter and impact the policy process because "what nursing is said to be constitutes what nursing is" (Kelly, Fealy, & Watson, 2011, p. 1804). Negative, demeaning, or powerless images of nurses have another negative impact, that of nurse invisibility in the marketing materials or web presence of many medical facilities (Carty, Coughlin, Kasoff, & Sullivan, 2000). Such invisibility does not socialize nurses to consider roles of *public ambassador* for a political cause.

Strategies Toward Becoming a Confident Public Ambassador for Nursing

Fortunately, there are effective strategies to create a core of confidence that supports the role of nurse as an effective political agent. A sound starting place is the identification of powerful examples or models of effective political force in action.

LEARNING FROM DISTANT OTHERS

Although there are many examples of politically powerful men to consider as potential role models—or behavior and styles you wish to avoid—politically powerful women represent a smaller proportion of the politically powerful. Regardless of alignment with your personal politics, individuals like Angela Merkel, Germany's first woman prime minister; Janet Yellen, first woman U.S. Federal Reserve chief; Dilma Rousseff, the president of Brazil; Condoleezza Rice; and Hillary Clinton, to name but a few, offer examples of women in power, worthy of study. Moreover, it is useful to identify individuals who mirror your race, ethnicity, gender, and—if possible—age, and then study strengths you admire as models to emulate. What qualities make them effective in the political arena? How did they become who they are? What skills did they develop, and what experiences fostered that skill development? How and when did they layer in parenting and partnering? What lessons about the navigation of personal and professional life can be gleaned? Biographies, autobiographies, and documentaries can offer useful illustrations.

LEARNING FROM AT-HAND MENTORS

Useful as it is to study the biographies, history, and style of influential women and men, a more immediate role model may be found in a mentor or collection of mentors, all of whom have different backgrounds and skill sets from which you can identify examples you wish to follow to become your best self. Although the professional and popular literature frequently touts the mentor route, an effective mentor–mentee relationship is not automatic or easy and must meet the needs of both the mentor and protégée. Box 11.2 outlines essential elements of effective mentoring, based on a qualitative study of 117 dyads.

Box 11.2

Elements of an Effective Mentoring Relationship

Effective Mentoring
Open communication and accessibility
Goals and challenges
Passion and inspiration
Caring personal relationship
Mutual respect and trust
Exchange of knowledge
Independence and collaboration
Role modeling

Source: Sanzero Eller, Lev, and Feurer (2013).

Unlike the exploration and potential applications of skills viewed at a distance in leaders, the mentor–mentee dynamic is an actual relationship and, like any relationship, takes work and compatibility. In addition, although the mentor's role is to help the mentee create a larger vision of what is possible for himself or herself and then fulfill the promise of that extended self, some mentors become caught in their own needs, for example, the need to be the rescuer and thus foster a codependent relationship (Kets de Vries, 2013). Eby (2007) further notes that relational problems such as personality clashes, jealousy, and unwillingness to learn may mar the mentoring and undermine growth potential. Similarly, if goals are not met, interaction costs may leave the mentor or mentee feeling the outcomes are not worth the effort. Seek out those with admirable political skills and become an apprentice. If mentors are easily identified, this approach can augment what can be learned from world and historical figures.

Thought Questions

1. What qualities make an individual an effective ambassador for a cause? How can essential skills be practiced?

2. What bills of interest to nurses are under consideration in the current or last state legislative session in your state?

3. How would you advise nurses who are interested in creating a political learning agenda for themselves? What sources of information and connection can you advise them to explore? What else would you need to know to help them?

4. Define the following key terms:

Advocate	Grassroots lobbying
Call to action	How a bill becomes a law
Crossover	Lobbyist
Direct lobbying	Political action committee
Get-out-the-vote efforts	Talking points

Exercise

1. Create a presentation for your peers that details the political process in your state. Include tangible suggestions for how to become involved.

2. Consider exemplary political role models. What skills do you share with them? What are your growth edges?

Quiz

TRUE OR FALSE

1. All advocacy is lobbying.

2. Grassroots lobbying can only be done by registered lobbyists.

3. Unusual alliances among groups to advocate on behalf of a particular bill or issue usually is looked on with suspicion by policymakers and should therefore be avoided.

4. Once introduced into the legislature, a bill draft rarely changes.

5. A foundational strategy to influence policy is to vote.

6. Political action committees have been deemed illegal in the United States since 1992.

7. Ethical guidelines may prohibit lobbyists from giving gifts to policymakers.

8. Bill drafts are vetted by the full Senate or House of Representatives before being reviewed by the appropriate committee.

9. Political action is inconsistent with the roles and responsibilities of the professional nurse.

10. Personality clashes, jealousy, and unwillingness to learn can mar the mentor–mentee relationship.

MULTIPLE CHOICE

11. One strategy to support political campaigns is
    A. Fund-raising for worthy candidates
    B. Working on *get-out-the-vote* efforts
    C. Both A and B
    D. Neither A nor B

12. Lobbyists
    A. Have the moral responsibility to present their personal view on an issue
    B. Do not need to be registered in the state
    C. Both A and B
    D. Neither A nor B

13. Ways to influence policymakers include
    A. Phone calls to the policymaker's office or staff
    B. E-mails to the policymaker's office or staff
    C. Both A and B
    D. Neither A nor B

14. An effective mentor–mentee relationship requires
    A. Collaboration
    B. Independence
    C. Both A and B
    D. Neither A nor B

NOTE

1. Shapiro (2008) offers that although associated with Bismarck starting in the 1930s, the original quote was coined in 1869 by lawyer-poet John Godfrey Saxe, who was cited in *The Daily Cleveland Herald* on March 29, 1869, as stating, "Laws , like sausage, cease to inspire respect in proportion as we know how they are made."

REFERENCES

Carty, B., Coughlin, C., Kasoff, J., & Sullivan, B. (2000). Where is the nursing presence on the medical center's website? *The Journal of Nursing Administration 30*(12), 569–570.

Des Jardin, K. E. (2001a). Political involvement in nursing—Politics, ethics, and strategic action. *Association of Operating Room Nurses Journal, 74*(5), 614–618, 621–622.

Des Jardin, K. E. (2001b). Political involvement in nursing—Education and empowerment. *Association of Operating Room Nurses Journal, 74*(4), 468–475.

Eby, L. (2007). Understanding relational problems in mentoring: A review and proposed investment model. In B. Ragins & L. Kran (Eds.), *The handbook of mentoring at work: Theory, research, and practice.* Thousand Oaks, CA: Sage.

Gordon, S. (2005). *Nursing against the odds: How health care cost-cutting, medical stereotypes, and medical hubris undermine nursing and patient care.* Ithaca, NY: Cornell University Press.

Health Resources and Services Administration. (2013). *The U.S. nursing workforce: Trends in supply and education.* Rockville, MD: Author.

Kelly, J., Fealy, G., & Watson, R. (2011). The image of you: Constructing nursing identities in YouTube. *Journal of Advanced Nursing, 68*(8), 1804–1813. doi:10.1111/j.1365-2648.2011.05872.x

Kets de Vries, M. F. R. (2013). The dangers of codependent mentoring [Blog post]. *Harvard Business Review.* Retrieved June 20, 2014, from http://blogs.hbr.org/2013/12/the-dangers-of-codependent-mentoring/

Pulcini, J. (2014). Interview with a nursing policy leader: A hopeful look at a changing profession. *American Journal of Nursing, 114*(1), 19–22. doi:10.1097/01.NAJ.0000441785.39914.ea

Robeznieks, A. (2014). AMA to Joint Commission: We're the head of the medical household. *Modern Healthcare.* Retrieved June 10, 2014, from www.modernhealthcare.com/article/20140610/NEWS/306109947

Sanzero Eller, L., Lev, E., & Feurer, A. (2013). Key components of an effective mentoring relationship: A qualitative study. *Nurse Education Today, 34*, 815–820.

Shapiro, F. (2008). Quote…misquote. *The New York Times.* Retrieved June 20, 2014, from www.nytimes.com/2008/07/21/magazine/27wwwl-guestsafire-t.html?_r=0

Summers, S., & Summers, H. J. (2010). *Saving lives: Why the media's portrayal of nurses puts us all at risk.* New York, NY: Kaplin.

EPILOGUE: REFLECTIONS ON LIVING AND LEADING IN A CHANGING NURSING WORLD

TELL ME ONE MORE TIME: WHAT DOES ALL THIS FINANCING, ECONOMICS, AND POLICY HAVE TO DO WITH NURSING?

Throughout this text we have navigated complex terrain that at one time was the domain of physicians, financial officers, chief executive officers (CEOs), and a very few nurse leaders and graduate students in nursing. We have explored policy and boardrooms, individual and population ethics, and health and payment reform, to name but a few tours on our journey to an expanded sense of professional self. This stretch can create an ache, yet it is necessary. The image of what it means to be a nurse is being rewritten because society needs what nurses know, yet too often what nurses know has been bound by stereotypical roles and images.

The very metaphor of nursing is that of a personal relationship, with one meaning of the term literally referring to a mother nourishing a child. These personal, intimate images create a confining narrative of what it means to be a nurse in our contemporary culture. A focus on care of an individual patient is valuable in some instances, but it is not enough to fully serve society. More is needed of nurses, of each and every one of us. Society needs nursing intelligence, and finance, economics, and policy are tools with particular impact when in the hands of a nurse. A traditional story illustrates this well.

Imagine you are sitting on a beach, sunning. You hear shouts from the water and realize that someone has gone under! Hero that you are, you leap into the water, pull the person ashore, and revive the person to then receive eternal thanks. "Ah, what a good day," you muse, "I saved a life." Tired, you fall asleep on the shore.

But wait, could it be? Now you are startled to hear not one, but two shouts! Drained but undaunted, you hold one person in each arm as you swim with your feet and torso. You perform serial resuscitation, and miraculously, both are fine, thanking you profusely.

Exhausted but pleased with your superhuman day's work, you fall asleep, only to hear shouts from the water yet again. Now there are four people in trouble! So weary, but always a nurse of ingenuity, you leap into the water, make a human chain of each of the individuals, pull them to shore, and again resuscitate all four. Wow! What a day! Now, completely spent, you are lulled asleep in the warm summer sun, content in your virtue and skill.

But no! You are stunned to hear a cacophony of shouts and splashes, and look to see the enormous bay full of people, all drowning, all screaming for help. Appalled, you know you will not be able to help them and will certainly drown trying. You instead decide a new approach is needed. "That's it," you declare. "I'm going upstream to see why people fall into the water in the first place."

Health policy is about going upstream. And, just like backhoes and forklifts in river engineering, finance and economics are simple tools that can help you do complex things. You can redesign the health care river ... and keep people from falling in.

It can feel very gratifying to care for individual patients, one by one. It can feel heroic. Indeed, it is why many of us became nurses. At the same time, there are only so many lives we can touch one by one. Policy is one tool to shape the top of the river, change the course, so people do not fall in. And finance and policy are key tools in the engineering redesign. It feels virtuous and certain to help individuals one by one, just like the nurse in the beach scenario. The work of policy and politics can feel less immediately gratifying—we cannot even see the lives we are touching—and less staunchly certain. It requires speaking up and speaking out, even when we cannot be sure that our policy change will be the right one. It requires a tolerance for ambiguity.

HOW TO RETAIN AND EXPAND ON WHAT YOU HAVE LEARNED

Now that you have the basics down, you have the canvas to create a deep and rich professional landscape. There is no better way to continue to grow than by applying these materials in everyday life. Board or politics experience is one way, but so, also, is teaching. By teaching others, so too, you yourself will learn. Questions from others cause us to pause and question ourselves, and in so doing, we grow. As Einstein famously stated, "If you can't explain it simply, you don't understand it well enough." Struggling to make things clear to others will help you to clarify them for yourself. Mentoring others is also a great way to learn. Let us imagine each of us hanging on to a steady hand above us, while we simultaneously provide that steady hand to another.

There are high-quality journals that are dedicated to health policy, for example, *Health Affairs*, which is written in a style that is understandable to an interdisciplinary audience. Major U.S. newspapers regularly highlight health, health care, and health policy. Consistent readership can help keep you abreast of thoughts and concerns your patients might be having.

Another important vehicle for staying current is your professional nursing organization. There are many nursing groups in which you might find meaningful membership. The American Nurses Association and its local state chapters typically also have a student group. This is a good place to begin practicing your leadership skills. There are also specialty organizations that may be of particular interest to the practicing nurse. Take the time to check out the options, read their mission statements, and then join those that feel like the best fit for you. And yes, joining costs money. That contribution to health, health care, and nursing is part of the obligation of being a professional. Even if you do not always have time to be involved directly, your financial support of these groups can help ensure that your cause is articulated in policy and political arenas.

Finally, lifelong learning is an essential element of the previously discussed ethical principle of role fidelity. To be faithful to the role of the nurse— and the responsibility we have to the public— we must continue to grow and learn. Usually, this is a bit uncomfortable because it feels safer to stay in the solid spot of what we know well, or think we know well, rather than alighting on the shifting ground of new learning. It can also be difficult to learn new things because they conflict with what we think we already knew. The idea that *learning is fun* just does not always hold. Learning is a struggle; *knowing is fun*. To be the nurse who can see new ways of doing things and enact change: *This* is fun. To midwife, a sound policy change that impacts hundreds, thousands, or even millions of people is delicate but gratifying work: *This* is fun. Both formal education in graduate school and informal education through conferences and webinars are part of lifelong learning. Ongoing, continuous learning is part of your future.

So, what will health care look like in a decade? A century? This is not fully clear, but one thing is clear. It will not look as it is today, and you can—and should—be part of the transformative process.

APPENDIX: QUIZ ANSWERS

Chapter 1	Chapter 2	Chapter 3
1. F	1. F	1. F
2. T	2. F	2. F
3. F	3. F	3. T
4. F	4. T	4. T
5. F	5. T	5. F
6. T	6. T	6. T
7. T	7. T	7. T
8. F*	8. T	8. T
9. T	9. T	9. T
10. T	10. F	10. T
11. D	11. B	11. B
12. A	12. B	12. C
13. A	13. D	13. C
14. C	14. C	14. C
15. D	15. C	15. C
16. B	16. B	16. C
17. D	17. D	17. D
18. A	18. A	18. D

*Note, the first part of Question 8 is true: Since the passage of the Affordable Care Act, children can stay on their parent's health insurance until age 26. The second part of the question is not true: Children can stay on their parent's insurance up to age 26 even if they are not dependents, not in school, and even if they are married.

Chapter 4	Chapter 5	Chapter 6
1. T	1. T	1. F
2. T	2. T	2. T
3. T	3. F	3. T
4. F	4. F	4. T
5. T	5. F	5. T
6. T	6. F	6. T
7. F	7. T	7. T
8. F	8. F	8. T
9. T	9. T	9. A
10. F	10. T	10. D
11. C	11. A	11. C
12. A	12. C	12. C
13. C	13. B	
14. C	14. A	
15. C	15. C	
16. C		

Chapter 7	Chapter 8	Chapter 9
1. F	1. T	1. F
2. F	2. T	2. F
3. T	3. F	3. T
4. F	4. T	4. F
5. T	5. T	5. T
6. T	6. F	6. T
7. T	7. T	7. F
8. T	8. T	8. F
9. F	9. T	9. F
10. T	10. F	10. F
11. C	11. A	11. C
12. C	12. B	12. A
13. B	13. C	13. D
14. B	14. A	14. C
15. A	15. B	15. C

Chapter 10

1. T
2. F
3. T
4. F
5. T
6. T
7. T
8. F
9. T
10. T
11. C
12. D
13. B
14. B
15. C

Chapter 11

1. F
2. F
3. F
4. F
5. T
6. F
7. T
8. F
9. F
10. T
11. C
12. D
13. C
14. C

GLOSSARY

Accountable care organization (ACO) Emerging from a provision of the Affordable Care Act, an ACO is a voluntary coalition of health care providers who accept health care and financial responsibility for a group of patients, the latter also referred to as *attributed lives* (see *attribution*).

Ad hoc Concerned or dealing with a specific, time-limited purpose or issue.

Administrative rule Guidelines developed by an administrative agency that elaborate the requirement of a law. Once promulgated, administrative rules have the power of laws.

Agenda An outline or plan of items to be discussed and possibly voted on at a meeting.

All payer Inclusive of commercial insurance, Medicare, and Medicaid.

Antitrust Legislation to prevent monopolies, with the intention of fostering competition.

Asymmetry A lack of equivalence or equality among parts.

Attribution The assignment of a provider who is responsible for the cost and quality of care for a patient, whether the patient sees that provider or not.

Audit A formal examination of accounts or records for the purpose of verification.

Autonomy Independence or freedom to choose and self-determine.

Beneficence The act of doing good.

Bundled payment In health care, bundling refers to reimbursement for a set of services or episodes of care rather than each unit of care provided.

Capitation From the Latin work *caput* meaning *head*; capitation means "by head," referring to a fixed payment for each person, regardless of the amount of services used.

Certificate of Need (CON) State program to control the growth of health care facilities or services and the associated cost of such growth.

Commodity An article of trade, such as grain or special metals, in contrast to a service.

Consumer price index (CPI) Measure of the prices paid by urban consumers for a representative set of services and goods.

Copayment A fixed amount a patient contributes each time any health services are used, often at the initial time of each health care service encounter. Copayments are waived for some preventative and early detection health services.

Cost sharing In health care, a contractual requirement that the patient bear at least some cost when seeking and using health care services. Examples include copayments and deductibles (see *copayment*; *deductible*).

Covenant A contract, agreement, or commitment.

Deductible An amount of money determined by insurance contract that must be expended by an individual or family before the insurance company provides reimbursement for health care services obtained.

Dehumanize To remove or deprive of human qualities or characteristics.

Deontology The branch of ethics that considers moral obligations and duty to create right action.

Determinant A determining factor.

Digitize The conversion of information, images, or sounds into a digital form that can be processed by a computer.

Dilemma A situation that demands a choice between equally undesirable alternatives.

Disparity A difference rooted in inequality or injustice.

Economics A science with many branches that is concerned with the production, distribution, and consumption of services and material goods.

Electronic health record (EHR) Digitized health and clinical data replacing paper charts, which allow information to be shared more easily among providers of patient care (see *digitize*).

Entitlement The right to a set of guaranteed benefits or compensation.

Ethics A system of principles to guide moral action.

Ethinomics   The intersection of ethics and economics, particularly as it relates to policy formation.

Everyday ethics   Ethical challenges encountered in unremarkable or ordinary, daily events or circumstances.

Ex officio   By virtue of a position, role, or office.

Expenditure   The act of expending or using something, particularly financial resources.

Federally qualified health center (FQHC)   Organizations receiving grants under the Public Health Service Act; FQHCs receive enhanced reimbursement from Medicare and Medicaid and must serve underserved areas and meet other conditions.

Fee-for-service   Health care reimbursement schema in which each element of service is unbundled from the whole into individual units of procedure and charged for separately (in contrast, see *bundled payment*).

Fidelity   Loyalty, faithfulness, and strict observance.

Financing   The act, process, or mechanism to obtain money.

Fringe benefits   Benefits received by an employee that are provided in additional to regular pay.

Gatekeeper   A health care provider, typically primary care, who is the first line of access to the health care system and who also controls referral to a specialist for that patient.

In network   In health care, a group of providers who have contracted with the patient's insurance company for reimbursement at a negotiated, typically lower, reimbursement rate (contrast with *out of network*).

Intergenerational   Between different generations or age cohorts.

Knowledge worker   Employee whose responsibilities are largely the creation, distribution, or application of knowledge.

Laissez-faire   The system or practice of noninterference, derived from the French term for *let (them) act*.

Legislative crossover   A designated date when a bill introduced in one chamber of the state legislature passes to the other for review, for example, a House bill "crosses over" to the Senate.

Liability   The situation of being accountable for something, especially legal responsibility.

Lobbyist   An individual hired for a cause or business to persuade policy-makers to support that cause or business.

Mandate   A command, requirement, or authoritative order.

Market Basket Index   The measure of how much more or less it costs to buy a set of goods and services in comparison to the amount in a base period.

Mentor   A knowledgeable, experienced advisor and guide.

Monopoly   Exclusive control of a product, supply, or trade of a service or commodity.

Moral   Concerned with the distinction between right and wrong conduct, and goodness or badness of human character.

Nonmaleficence   Avoidance of harm.

Out of network   In health care, providers who have not contracted with an individual's insurance company for a negotiated rate.

Pay for performance (P4P)   Reimbursement in addition to traditional fee-for-service that is received for reaching defined quality metrics.

Per diem   By the day, or, for each day.

Per member per month (PMPM)   Reimbursement strategy in which the provider organization receives a fixed sum of money each month for each patient enrollee, regardless of the amount of services used or unused.

Philanthropy   Charitable giving for a particular cause or organization.

Political action committee (PAC)   An issues-oriented group that raises money and contributes to political campaigns and candidates who support its issues.

Premium   In insurance, an amount to be paid for coverage under a contract, typically in monthly increments.

Quaternary   Fourth in order.

Quorum   The required number of group members needed to conduct group business.

Reimbursement   Payment for services provided.

Reserve   Financial resources held aside to be used for future financial demands, both expected and unexpected.

Risk adjusted   An approach that accounts for differing severity of patients' conditions to enable fair cost, utilization, and quality comparisons among organizations and other providers.

Self-rationing   Self-imposed restrictions on purchasing goods or using services.

Statute   A law enacted by a legislative body and expressed in a formal document.

Subsidy   Financial assistance provided by a governmental entity.

Superutilizer   Individual, typically with complex health and social issues, who uses disproportionately high levels of health care, including emergency departments and hospitals.

Surplus   The amount of money that remains above what is needed or used.

Sustainability   The ability to be continued and ongoing.

Tertiary   Third in order.

Throughput   Derived from the phrase "put through"; the amount of material or number of individuals who can be moved through a process in a given time.

Transparent   Undisguised or unconcealed, easy to perceive.

Universal   Characteristic of or applicable to all.

Upcoding   To inaccurately assign a medical billing code to increase or maximize the amount of reimbursement received.

Utilitarianism   The branch of ethics that considers utility, promoting the greatest amount of good or happiness for the greatest number of people.

Virtue   Behavior that shows moral excellence (see *moral,* Chapter 7).

INDEX